sophie braimbridge

stylish mediterranean *in minutes*

photography by Manos Chatzikonstantis

kyle books

sophie braimbridge

stylish mediterranean

in minutes

Dedication

To Ab my husband, and his office, for having the difficult task of eating all my tested recipes. It was a hard job! And to my two daughters, Ella and Lula, who have to put up with their mother!

This edition publilshed in 2007 by Kyle Books
An imprint of Kyle Cathie Limited
www.kylecathie.com

Distributed by National Book Network
4501 Forbes Boulevard, Suite 200
Lanham, MD 20706
(301) 459 3366

ISBN (13-digit) 978 1 904920 56 4

Design © 2006 Kyle Cathie Limited
Text © 2006 by Sophie Braimbridge
Photography © 2006 by Manos Chatzikonstantis

Design and Art Direction Geoff Hayes
Photography Manos Chatzikonstantis
Project Editor Stephanie Evans
Props styling Michail Touros
Home economists Caroline Elwood , Lizzie Harris and Lou Mackaness
Production Sha Huxtable & Alice Holloway

Sophie Braimbridge is hereby identified as the author of this work in accordance with Section 77 of the Copyright, Designs and Patents Act 1988.

Braimbridge, Sophie
Stylish Mediterranean in Minutes/Sophie Braimbridge.
1. Cookery, Mediterranean
Library of Congress Number: 2006936119

Color reproduction by Sang Choy International
Printed in Singapore by Star Standard

Acknowledgements
I would like to acknowledge the many suppliers who managed to track down or deliver such great produce to make this book a real treat to accomplish. So thank you to Andreas Georgiou Fruit and Vegetables, Jarvis Fish, Jeffries Butchers, Sud Ovest Delicatessen and Vallebona.

Picture acknowledgements for chapter openers: 10-11, Henry Fonda, Archivio Toscani/Alinari Archives—Florence; 32-33: Jean-Paul Belmondo & Henri Verneuil, The Kobal Collection/Mirkine; 46-47: *La Guerisseur*, Ronald Grant Archive: 60-61: Ugo Tognazzi, The Kobal Collection/Mirkine; 78-79: Bert Hardy/Stringer/Getty Images; 90-91: *Soltanto un Bacio*, Maladini Collection/Alinari Archives—Florence; 104-105: *Il Seduttore*, Ronald Grant Archive; 130-131: *La Grande Bouffe*, Mara/Capitolina/The Kobal Collection; 148-149: Brigette Bardot & Roger Vadin, Hulton/Deutsch Collection/CORBIS

contents

Introduction   6

Chapter 1   **Hors d'oeuvres, tapas, antipasti, mezze**   10

Chapter 2   **Soups and sauces**   32

Chapter 3   **Salads**   46

Chapter 4   **Pasta, rice, and legumes**   60

Chapter 5   **Egg and cheese dishes**   78

Chapter 6   **Vegetables**   90

Chapter 7   **Fish**   104

Chapter 8   **Meat and poultry**   130

Chapter 9   **Desserts**   148

Index   159

introduction

The Mediterranean region is shared by many countries that may be physically and culturally different and yet show similarities, not least in terms of their food. They enjoy an abundance of products, fished from the sea itself, of course, but also ripened under sunny skies in the fertile soils that surround it. During my travels I've discovered how a great number of ingredients are used in varying and innovative ways in all these countries. The ubiquitous tomato, originally from South America, is now a staple throughout the region. (And I mean flavorsome tomatoes, ripened on the vine under a gloriously hot sun, not your tasteless, watery greenhouse specimen!) It features in so many recipes, along with garlic, eggplant, and olive oil... quintessential Mediterranean ingredients.

Invasion and integration

A dip into the Mediterranean past reveals how conquering nations have influenced the cuisine of the occupied countries. The connecting sea meant that no country or island was isolated from its neighbors. The food of southern Spain and Sicily, for example, is still dominated by Arab spices and flavors such as saffron, dates, and pomegranates introduced by the Moors; Morocco exhibits a strong French influence; while central European countries, such as Croatia and Slovenia, have similarities with Italian cuisine. This intermingling of cultures around the Mediterranean region is as compelling to the cook as to the traveler or the historian.

The single unifying theme for this book must be the sea. Each time I prepare one of these recipes it conjures up the life around this bountiful sea. I get an instant recall of any number of beautiful images, such as the hundreds of candles lit to celebrate a saint's day in a small bay in Sicily, or the towering sight of the giant ships in Istanbul docks. Or the gold-encrusted turrets of the mosques and the jewel-bright tiles that seem to adorn every manmade surface in Morocco, the simple dazzling-white buildings that dot the Greek islands, the mouthwatering pastel tones that accent the architecture in towns and cities in the south of France and Spain. There are smells and sounds too: aromas emanating from street stalls cooking irresistible snacks, the cheerful banter in bars, restaurants and colorful markets, the quayside auction of the day's catch, the call to prayer... And of course, there's the abiding memory of the warmth and light of the sun itself that make dining al fresco such a cherished pleasure the length and breadth of the Mediterranean. The cafe culture must have been invented somewhere along these balmy shores.

What's on the menu?

The heat of the sun combined with the wealth of the sea makes for a stunning range of food: freshly landed seafood and fish, mouthwatering salads, vegetables, and fruit. But it's not all about summer cool. For those months when the tourist crowds have long departed, there are also rich stews and simply grilled meats to warm you from within. Simplicity is the word here. With such a vast collection of fresh ingredients at hand, cooks can rely on the quality rather than time spent in the kitchen making over-elaborate foods. Preparation and cooking are simple too. A few decent saucepans and a skillet, a gratin dish and a heavy-bottomed casserole, a mortar and pestle or spice grinder, and a couple of good knives for chopping vegetables and herbs and smashing garlic will suffice.

The Mediterranean climate does not lend itself to rich pasture for dairy herds to produce copious amounts of cream and butter. Red meat is not a big part of the diet, either. The emphasis is on fruit and vegetables, easily grown in the long months of sunshine. It's now recognized as one of the healthiest diets in the world. The soils may be rich but the terrain is often rugged and water supply critical. The dry conditions are more suited to sheep and goats, whose milk produces light cheeses such as feta and manchego, and to pigs, whose meat makes the many cured hams, sausages, and salamis. Poultry can scratch a living almost anywhere, and not just chicken but quail and pigeon, too. Fruit and nut trees—orange, lemon, peach, almond, and walnut—are much at home on the sun-baked slopes. Grapevines flourish, and their fruit, fresh, or fermented as wine or spirits, happily partners the delights on the Mediterranean table. And the crop of the ancient olive groves provides yet another reason why the food of this region is so in tune with modern life: it's fresh and healthy.

The daily bread

Bread is an integral part of the Mediterranean meal. It commands huge respect and is not to be squandered—hence the many recipes using leftover bread. You'll find it in every shape and size: thin sticks including grissini, or round and long such as French baguette or Italian ciabatta. There are round or oblong flatbreads—pita from Turkey or Greece and very large flat sheets called lavash in Lebanon. The Sardinians may have the thinnest of all, like a poppadom. Among the thicker, denser "country-style" breads are sour-doughs. Here the raising agent is not commercial yeast but "homegrown", called an appetizer, created by fermenting fruits, vegetables, or alcohol.

Bread is served in all manner of ways—warm and fresh from the oven, broiled, or baked from scratch in front of your eyes in the small oven in restaurants or outside ovens. It may also turn up as breadcrumbs, soaked in oil and mixed in salads or sauces as a binding agent, or broiled and refreshed with toppings or dips.

Ready in half an hour

The Mediterranean emphasis on fresh, quality ingredients, minimal preparation, and simple cooking methods sums up my style of cooking: light, easy recipes that will delight friends and family, weekdays or weekends. My task is to prepare and cook traditional and unusual dishes in less than 30 minutes. It's not at all difficult to keep within this time limit—just follow my method for preparing ingredients while you cook.

I've organized my chapters on Mediterranean principles. The emphasis is on lots of little dishes to serve as snacks or appetizers. Salads and vegetables are loosely defined here: you'll find salads that are warm or use cooked vegetables, and vegetable dishes that are dressed or marinated like a salad. Fish and Seafood, and Pasta, Rice, and Legumes are (as you'd expect) significant sections. With judicious use of the right herbs, spices, and sauces, simple, readily available ingredients translate into truly memorable meals. You'll see that meat is used sparingly: another reflection of the healthy Mediterranean diet. A little alcohol in the pan lifts the humblest slice of liver (and the bottle won't be wasted: try a shot of Marsala or grappa with your dessert). Desserts are usually fruit-based and there are some delicious ways of serving it: broiled, sautéed, marinated.

Inside the Mediterranean larder

We're now in the habit of using sea salt and freshly ground pepper for maximum flavor. Mediterraneans also use salted anchovies as much as a seasoning as an ingredient. It's well worth keeping anchovy fillets in the cupboard. Citrus fruits—lemons especially—are similarly used to enhance the flavors on your plate. This may be the zest and juice in the dish, a simple wedge for squeezing, or a preserved lemon which you can find in Middle Eastern food stores. They, along with tamarind, add a real tang to southern Mediterranean dishes. Tamarind is a legume, a distant cousin of the fava bean. A sharp-tasting purée is made from the sticky flesh around the seeds which adds a complex sweet-sour flavor to a dish. Tamarind is now widely available in jars (I find the one that resembles black too bitter:

look for the dark orange-brown variety) but if you can only find packets with the seeds and fiber attached, soak the sticky flesh in a small amount of warm water then use just the soaking liquid.

More stylish still is the use of pomegranates, not only the jewel-like pink seeds, which pop up in salads and sauces, but also a concentrated syrup which you can buy in specialty food stores. This, like tamarind, adds a sweet-sour pungency to sugar or sweet foods. And then there's sumac, another spice that might seem unusual to a lot of cooks but one that is used throughout the southern Mediterranean region. The red seeds of sumac come ready ground and add a sour flavor to a recipe, similar to a tangy lemon taste. This spice is less easy to track down but some good supermarkets do now stock it as well as Middle Eastern stores. It is found most famously in Fattoush (Lebanese bread salad, see page 52 for the recipe), although it also works very well in a marinade for meat.

Another ingredient I would urge you to seek out is bottarga, which is much used in Italian recipes. Bottarga is cured mullet or tuna roe, grated over pasta like Parmesan, but also served over eggs or even on toast. I find the mullet roe less pungent and have seen it in dried flake form in good supermarkets, although if you can track some fresh from a good Italian deli or food supplier you will get a more authentic flavor.

There is a whole range of Mediterranean herbs. Flatleaf parsley and thyme are ubiquitous but other herbs are identified with certain cuisines. Oregano, for example, mostly features in Italian dishes and we think of chervil, dill, and tarragon as French. Yet Lebanese cooking includes tarragon, as do recipes from parts of Spain, and dill is found throughout Turkey, Lebanon, and Syria. But you would never see dill or cilantro in Italy, nor use basil in Turkish cooking. Similarly, rosemary or sage rarely go beyond Greece as a cooking ingredient.

The Mediterraneans never seem to lose their ability to feel passionate about the quality of their food, and they are happy to spend time shopping in markets or at local stalls, to get the best from their suppliers. It shows their confidence in what they want, which—to a chef—is most appealing. Or is it because, as a Lebanese saying goes, "the more eggplant dishes you learn to cook the longer you keep your husband?" Even if that's the last thing on your mind, enjoy the recipes in this book!

hors d'oeuvres, tapas, antipasti, mezze

This chapter epitomizes the essence of the Mediterranean way with food. Tasty little morsels are served throughout the region as a way to start a meal or whet the appetite. The ritual of "breaking bread" is done so stylishly here—it's an integral part of Mediterranean life. The term doesn't simply refer to the physical action, be it from a French baguette, toasted slices rubbed with garlic, crunchy breadsticks, warm pita, or flatbread. It's as much a phrase used to invite friends and family to share in a pleasurable and essential experience. I hope you can almost feel the warmth and hear the sound of laughter and chatting, loud shouts—even screams—from a heated debate, amid the general jolly conviviality as I show you the many delicious recipes that hallmark the countries around the Mediterranean.

How a meal begins is really important to set the taste buds alight. To be offered an array of beautifully prepared taste sensations is, therefore, a great way to start. The Spanish probably have the most famous of this section: tapas. The tapa is almost an institution throughout Spain: people will stop off after work for tapas and there are restaurants that entirely dedicate themselves to serving these snacks. But "snack" is probably far too demeaning a term for these irresistible bites. The French call them hors d'oeuvres; to the Italians they are antipasti; and from Greece to Syria they are known as mezze. Preparing a few of these recipes, alternating between the simplest and the more involved, will earn you praise and guarantee you don't spend too much time in the kitchen.

smoked eggplant purée
(baba ghanoush)

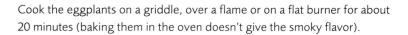

SERVES 4
PREPARATION TIME 10 MINUTES COOKING TIME 20 MINUTES

This is a classic Turkish dish served as a mezze. I wanted to include this recipe because the eggplant is broiled whole which gives a creamy, smoky flavor that is so prevalent in the region's cuisine. But to broil them within my 30-minute rule you'll need smallish eggplants, weighing around 8 ounces each—larger ones will just take longer to broil. Serve as part of a selection of mezze with warm bread or as a dip with raw vegetables.

2 medium eggplants (1 pound total weight)

1 teaspoon cumin seeds

1 large garlic clove, crushed with a pinch of salt

½ cup Greek-style yogurt

1 tablespoon tahini

2 tablespoons coarsely chopped flatleaf parsley

Sea salt and freshly ground black pepper

to garnish

paprika or pomegranate seeds

drizzle of extra virgin olive oil

Cook the eggplants on a griddle, over a flame or on a flat burner for about 20 minutes (baking them in the oven doesn't give the smoky flavor).

Meanwhile, toast the cumin gently in a dry frying pan for a few minutes then grind in a mortar and pestle or spice grinder.

When the eggplant is cooked, place them in a sieve over a bowl and leave for about 5 minutes to cool slightly and drain off any bitter juices. As soon as they are cool enough to handle, peel away the burned skin and break off the thorny stem. Return to the sieve and press down with a large metal spoon to drain off any remaining juices.

When the eggplant has drained, coarsely chop the flesh and mix together with the cumin, garlic, yogurt, tahini, parsley, and pepper. Taste and add more salt if necessary.

Garnish with a sprinkle of paprika or pomegranate seeds, drizzle with olive oil, and serve.

tuna tartare with crème fraîche and chervil

SERVES 2 AS AN APPETIZER, OR 4 LARGE CANAPÉS
PREPARATION TIME 15 MINUTES

Don't attempt this dish unless the fish is really fresh as it is served raw. If you can, buy sushi-grade tuna, which is intended to be eaten raw. Ask your fishmonger to slice the tuna very thinly. You can substitute fresh salmon, as this recipe works well with either. In the south of France there is plenty of tuna landed daily and although salmon is not a Mediterranean fish, the locals love to eat it! Salmon is more likely to be served in classy restaurants and reminds me of my earlier career in French kitchens in the early 90s. It tastes equally delicious—you can add a little fresh chopped ginger or pink peppercorns for an extra element. The other bit of advice is, don't be tempted to use a food processor. The fish will be masticated to an undesirable consistency. Serve the tartare on thin toast—ideally melba toast.

7 ounces tuna fillet

1 tablespoon very finely chopped scallion or shallot

½ teaspoon fennel seeds

1 tablespoon finely chopped chervil or dill

1 tablespoon lime or lemon juice

1 heaped tablespoon crème fraîche

Sea salt and freshly ground black pepper

Thin white toast to serve

To finely chop the tuna, you need a very sharp knife. Start by slicing it thinly, then cut into thin strips and finally dice the strips, giving a brief chop to the fish to ensure all pieces are separated. Place in a bowl.

Finely chop the scallion or shallot and grind the fennel seeds in a mortar and pestle or spice grinder. Finely chop the chervil or dill and add all three ingredients to the tuna along with the lime juice, crème fraîche, salt and pepper. Give the mixture a good stir and leave for 5–10 minutes or a little longer if you wish to infuse the flavors.

Serve chilled on toast.

chickpea fritters

MAKES 16–20 FRITTERS
PREPARATION TIME 5 MINUTES COOKING TIME 20 MINUTES
RESTING TIME 45 MINUTES

These little fritters go by various names (socca, panisses, panelle, farinata) and are found all over the Mediterranean, from France to Italy to Sicily and Tunisia. The perfect street food, they are made more like pancakes in Nice, sandwiched between bread in Sicily, or thinly poured and baked in Italy. I have stretched the concept of 30 minutes here because although they are very easy to make and quick to cook the batter needs a little time to cool down! You can add basil, parsley, or rosemary to the mixture.

1½ cups chickpea flour

3¼ cups water

1 tablespoon extra virgin olive oil plus extra for greasing

2 tablespoons chopped flatleaf parsley

Sea salt and freshly ground black pepper

1 cup olive oil

Put the flour into a medium saucepan and season with salt and pepper. Slowly add the water, mixing well with a whisk so there are no lumps. Place the pan on the heat and bring to a simmer, stirring all the time with a wooden spoon. Cook for 10 minutes. Add the tablespoon of oil and the parsley. Mix well.

Oil a 9-inch baking pan or rectangular gratin dish and pour in the batter—it will fill to about 1 inch deep. Spread out the mixture evenly and, if you're in a hurry, place outside to cool down.

When the mixture is firm, cut it into thick sticks.

Put the olive oil in a frying pan and heat to medium-high. Cook the fritters for about 2 minutes on each side, until golden brown, but still a little creamy inside when broken open.

Drain on paper towels and season with salt. Serve immediately, still warm and fresh from the pan—they're less good if left to cool down or reheated.

braised radicchio and smoked mozzarella bruschetta

SERVES 6
PREPARATION TIME 10 MINUTES COOKING TIME 15 MINUTES

I have also made this Italian dish with gorgonzola if you can't find smoked mozzarella. But reduce the amount to about 2½ ounces as gorgonzola is much stronger in flavor than mozzarella.

1 large head radicchio (about 10 ounces)

3 tablespoons extra virgin olive oil

1 tablespoon chopped thyme leaves

2 tablespoons red wine vinegar

1 heaped teaspoon sugar

6 slices sourdough or country-style bread

1 garlic clove

1 small smoked mozzarella (about 5 ounces)

Extra virgin olive oil, to drizzle

Sea salt and freshly ground black pepper

Preheat the broiler to high. Quarter the radicchio and discard the tough heart. Shred each quarter into thin slices.

Heat the olive oil in a large lidded saucepan over a medium heat. Add the raddichio and stir until it starts to wilt. Add the thyme, salt and pepper and cook for 2–3 minutes. Add the vinegar and sugar, cover the pan, and gently cook for about 10 minutes. Stir occasionally to prevent it from burning; you want the radicchio softened and the vinegar reduced. Remove the lid after about 5 minutes.

Toast the bread and while the slices are still hot rub with garlic. Keep warm on the pan.

Grate the mozzarella (or slice the gorgonzola if using). Divide the radicchio between the toast slices. Scatter over the cheese and broil on a high heat until the cheese has just melted, about 2 minutes.

Remove the bruschetta from the broiler and drizzle over a little olive oil. Serve immediately.

mozzarella and parmesan fritters

MAKES 10–12 FRITTERS
PREPARATION TIME 15 MINUTES COOKING TIME 5–10 MINUTES

I was served these fritters in Sicily with other antipasti—delicious! You can add chopped anchovies or olives, or serve them with tapenade (see page 117). You don't need a good-quality mozzarella as it's much wetter, which makes the fritters hard to prepare, and its delicate flavor will be lost when deep-fried. You can also substitute another Italian melting cheese, such as provolone. The fritters can be made a little in advance and kept warm in the oven but they are best eaten freshly made.

10 ounces firm mozzarella

1³/4-ounce piece of Parmesan cheese

1 large garlic clove, crushed with salt

1 heaped tablespoon chopped basil or rosemary

2 medium eggs

Scant ½ cup all-purpose flour

Sea salt and freshly ground black pepper

1 cup sunflower oil

Wrap the mozzarella in paper towels if the surface is at all wet. Then grate it on the large holes of a grater. Grate the Parmesan on the medium size tooth. Transfer both cheeses to a bowl. Add the crushed garlic, basil, eggs, flour, salt and pepper and mix well. Taste for correct seasoning.

Divide the mixture into about 10 pieces and shape them into balls the size of a golf ball, each about 1½ ounces. Press firmly to prevent them from falling apart then slightly flatten so they are easier to cook. Place on a plate. (They can be prepared in advance up to this stage and kept in the fridge but allow them to cook a little longer and more gently.)

Heat the oil in a large skillet over a medium-high heat. Don't let it smoke. Slide in a few fritters at a time and cook for up to 2 minutes on each side, or until golden brown, depending on how gooey you want the center. Once in the pan, don't try to move them for the first 2 minutes, after which they will be easier to remove with a metal spatula. Drain on paper towels while you continue to cook the remainder. Serve hot.

deep-fried sage leaves
with anchovies

MAKES 12 LARGE OR 24 MEDIUM SAGE PARCELS
PREPARATION TIME 15 MINUTES COOKING TIME 5 MINUTES

These are really delicious munched in the sun with a glass of really chilled white wine. Somehow, when I'm back home and it's cold, it's not quite the same, but these little nibbles will certainly keep guests content before your main meal. If you can get zucchini blossoms too, these work very well together. Anchovies tend to be salty, so you can always rinse them in cold water and drain them briefly before pressing between the sage leaves.

½ cup plus 2 tablespoons all-purpose flour

Dash of olive oil

Pinch of salt

½ cup plus 2 tablespoons warm water

1 egg white

12 anchovy fillets

24 large sage leaves

1 cup sunflower oil

Lemon wedges to serve

Put the flour in a bowl and make a well in the center. Pour in the olive oil, salt, and warm water. Slowly stir in the flour from the edges, so that it forms a paste with the consistency of thick runny cream.

Put the egg white in a clean, dry, small bowl and whisk for about 1 minute or until soft peaks form. Mix the white into the batter. Set aside.

Rinse the anchovies and dry on paper towels. Remove the sage leaves from the stems and sort into pairs, aiming to match their size if possible. If the sage leaves are large, use 1 anchovy fillet per pair. For smaller leaves you might need to cut each fillet in half.

Lay a sage leaf on a board, dark-colored side face up. Place the anchovy down the middle and press the other sage leaf, dark-colored side down. Press this little parcel together to seal the anchovy inside and lay flat.

Carefully pick up a sage parcel and, holding at the stem end, gently dunk into the batter to coat. Carefully release your fingers to ensure all of the parcel is covered. If it separates, just stick the parcel back together. Repeat the process with the remaining sage leaf parcels. (You may have some batter left over.) You can prepare up to this stage a little in advance if necessary.

Heat the sunflower oil in a skillet to medium-hot. Drop in a little batter and when just sizzling, start cooking the leaves. If the oil starts to smoke reduce the heat a little.

Cook the leaves for about 1 minute or less on each side, or until both sides are golden brown. Drain on paper towels and serve with a squeeze of lemon. Don't be tempted to salt them as the anchovies are salty enough.

Serve and eat immediately.

Tip: If you have an old saucepan you can turn it into a deep-fat fryer. Use a thermometer and wait for the oil to reach 180°C/350°F. Or heat the oil slowly and when a piece of bread sizzles vigorously and browns quite quickly, the oil is the right temperature.

tabbouleh

SERVES 4
PREPARATION TIME 20 MINUTES

This is a simple, healthy salad that is traditionally served as a mezze in Turkey and the Lebanon but it also partners well with plain broiled meat or fish. Bulgar or bulgur wheat is also known as cracked wheat. Wholemeal bulgar wheat is not only authentic but healthier, if you can find it. There are coarse and fine versions of bulgar wheat—use whichever you prefer. But the result should be more of a parsley salad with tiny flecks of wheat, not the other way round.

2 tablespoons bulgar wheat

4½ ounces fresh flatleaf parsley

2½ ounces fresh mint leaves

Juice of 1 large lemon

1 large tomato or 12 cherry tomatoes, finely diced

3 tablespoons extra virgin olive oil

Sea salt and freshly ground black pepper

Soak the bulgar wheat in just enough hot water to cover. Leave for 10 minutes and drain well, pressing out the water. Set aside.

Rinse the herbs and remove from the stem. Place in a salad spinner and dry well. Place on a dishcloth and leave to dry as much as possible, but be careful not to bruise the leaves or they will go brown and discolor the salad.

Once the herbs are dry, coarsely chop and place in a bowl. Add the drained bulgar wheat, lemon juice, diced tomatoes, olive oil, salt and pepper. Mix well. You can serve it immediately but it will keep for several hours and the flavors will infuse.

spanish tomato bread with manchego and olives

SERVES 4
PREPARATION TIME 10 MINUTES   COOKING TIME 5 MINUTES

Many countries have recipes that use leftover bread, often toasted and topped with vegetables, fish, or meat. Spain has one of the simplest variations on this theme: toasted slices rubbed with tomato. My friend Jake, from the restaurant Cigala in Lamb's Conduit Street in London, grates the flesh of a peeled tomato over the bread to enhance the flavor of the bread. You can increase the number of accompaniments you want to serve: Serrano ham and caperberries are two suggestions.

As with so many easy recipes, the taste is all about quality of ingredients. Manchego is a type of Spanish cheese made from sheep's milk. It is sold at different ages, from young to mature, therefore soft to hard. Sample several to choose the one you most like. Buy good-quality black or green olives. The best are marinated in olive oil. The worst are those left in brine with the stone removed. Spanish bread is often much lighter than Italian or French sourdough varieties, so when toasted it's is far crisper. The most authentic way to toast the bread is on a griddle.

8 slices good-quality Manchego cheese

4 tablespoons of good-quality whole olives

4 large slices country-style bread

1 garlic clove, peeled

1 ripe, tasty tomato

Good-quality extra virgin olive oil

Arrange the cheese and olives in bowls or on a plate.

Griddle the bread until just golden brown on both sides. Rub the bread while still hot with the garlic. Cut the tomato in half and generously rub the cut side over the bread to press as much of the tomato juice as possible onto the bread. Finally drizzle over the olive oil and cut in half at an angle. Serve the bread immediately so your guests can nibble on the cheese, olives and warm tomato toast. Perfect with a glass of dry sherry to start a meal.

marinated octopus salad

SERVES 4 AS AN APPETIZER OR TAPAS
PREPARATION TIME 10 MINUTES COOKING TIME 10 MINUTES
MARINATING TIME AT LEAST 10 MINUTES, PREFERABLY FOR
SEVERAL HOURS

Although octopus is quite hard to find in the U.S., it is sold everywhere in the Mediterranean and is quite delicious. A traditional way of serving octopus is as a salad, boiled first, then marinated (preferably for several hours). The longer it marinates the better the taste, so I have sneaked in this recipe as it's so prevalent throughout the region. It can be marinated just in oil and lemon, or with chili and parsley added. In Spain they include paprika, in Greece fennel seeds. See which you prefer. Try to buy small octopus, which are more tender, and ask your fishmonger to clean them by removing the innards, beak, and eyes.

1½ pounds small octopus, cleaned

1 tablespoon lemon juice or vinegar

1 bayleaf

4 peppercorns

for the marinade

6 tablespoons extra virgin olive oil

2 tablespoons lemon juice

Sea salt and freshly ground black pepper

to garnish

Sprinkling of paprika

2 tablespoons coarsely chopped flatleaf parsley

Rinse the octopus really well in cold water to remove any grit or dirt, particularly from the suckers, and pull off the skin if possible. Beat the octopus (against the kitchen sink will do) for a few minutes to tenderize the meat. Cut the tentacles into small strips or, if they are large, into disks about 1/4 inch thick.

Bring a saucepan of water infused with the lemon juice, bayleaf, and peppercorns to a simmer. Add the prepared octopus to the water and simmer gently for 10 minutes. Drain well.

Place the octopus in a bowl, mix with olive oil, lemon juice, salt and pepper. Leave to marinate for 10 minutes or longer if you can.

Just before serving, sprinkle with paprika and parsley. Serve with plenty of crusty bread.

vegetable platter with lavash and extra virgin olive oil

SERVES 4–6
PREPARATION TIME 15–20 MINUTES

This very simple but beautiful-looking mezze is often placed in front of you in Lebanon, Turkey, or Syria to start your meal, as the French would bring a basket of bread. Other times it can be a more substantial dish, and you might wish to serve it as an appetizer. The ingredients are just a guideline. Do adapt to what is fresh and available.

1 head romaine lettuce

Bunch of arugula

Bunch of mint

Bunch of basil

Bunch of cilantro

Bunch of dill

Bunch of radishes, trimmed (3 ounces)

2–3 small scallions, trimmed and halved lengthways

3 ounces small cherry tomatoes

2½ ounces walnuts, shelled

3½ ounces feta cheese, cubed

Good-quality extra virgin olive oil

Sea salt

3–4 large sheets lavash or pita bread

Carefully wash the lettuce and herbs. (I swing them over the sink to remove any excess water without crushing or bruising the leaves.) Wash the radishes and scallions and rinse the tomatoes. Leave everything to drain for a few minutes.

Select a large serving platter or tray. Cut the lettuce into long thin strips and arrange, with the herbs, on the platter. Top with the radishes, scallions, tomatoes, walnuts, and feta cheese. Pour the olive oil into one or two bowls for people to dip their ingredients into and offer round a little bowl of salt, too.

If using pita bread, warm it through but not lavash—it will be too crispy if heated first. Serve everything together, allowing people to eat bits of bread, with a little cheese, some salad and herb leaves, folded over and dunked in the oil. Or the vegetables and nuts can be just eaten whole.

prunes wrapped in bacon and stuffed with walnuts

MAKES ABOUT 24
PREPARATION TIME 10 MINUTES COOKING TIME 20 MINUTES

These are delicious as canapés, or hors d'oeuvres that the French started and the English adopted as devils on horseback. The fresh walnuts give them extra crunch. The weight of the ingredients is approximate as the size of each prune will affect the final amount, so buy a little more if the numbers are important.

8 ounces large soft pitted prunes

7 ounces fresh walnuts, or roasted almonds

12 slices smoked, rindless bacon

or thinly sliced pancetta

1 tablespoon rosemary, finely chopped

Drizzle of oil for roasting

Preheat the oven to 400°F.

Stuff the prunes with a half walnut. Cut the bacon slices in half making 24 short slices. Place 6 pieces of bacon on a work surface and stretch each piece lengthways. (If you like lots of bacon you could use the whole slice and increase the total number of slices.)

Sprinkle some rosemary over the bacon pieces, then place a stuffed prune at the bottom of each slice. Roll up the prune in the bacon. Repeat this process until the ingredients are used up. These can be prepared in advance and even frozen.

Cover a roasting pan with aluminum foil, drizzle with oil, and cook the prepared rolls for about 20–30 minutes until the bacon is crisp and golden brown.

Remove from the oven and set aside for 5 minutes before serving, as they will be very hot.

chicken livers, spinach, currants, and pinenuts on toast

MAKES 8 SMALL TOASTS, SERVES 4 AS AN APPETIZER
PREPARATION TIME 15 MINUTES COOKING TIME 15 MINUTES

Sicilian cuisine is heavily influenced by Arabic culinary traditions and the sweet flavor of currants with spinach is a classic combination.

4 tablespoons extra virgin olive oil

1 medium red onion, quartered and sliced

1³/4 ounces pinenuts

2 large garlic cloves

1³/4 ounces currants

1 pound washed and trimmed baby spinach

8 ounces chicken livers, trimmed

¹/2 cup Marsala (or sweet sherry or balsamic vinegar)

4 medium–large slices country-style bread

Extra virgin olive oil, to drizzle

Preheat the broiler to high. Put 3 tablespoons of the olive oil into a large lidded saucepan. Add the onions and pinenuts, cover and cook, stirring occasionally, for about 10 minutes on a medium-low heat, until the pinenuts are light golden brown and the onion is soft.

Meanwhile, toast the bread and while the slices are still hot rub with a whole garlic clove. Set aside on a plate and keep warm.

Chop the remaining garlic and add to the onion with the currants. Cook for a minute. Add the spinach and cook until just wilted, then set aside.

Meanwhile, heat a large skillet until hot. Add the remaining oil and cook the chicken livers on both sides for about 2 minutes in total. Season with salt and pepper then deglaze the pan with the Marsala. Cook for no more than a minute, then remove the livers. Add the spinach mixture to the pan and coat in the Marsala. Cook until all the juices are reduced.

To serve, put the spinach on the warm toasts and top with the chicken livers. Drizzle with a little extra olive oil and serve immediately.

carrot and tahini salad

SERVES 4–6
PREPARATION TIME 20 MINUTES

This is great served as part of a mezze with other Moroccan or Lebanese favorites such as falafel or smoked eggplant salad (see page 12). Sometimes I toast a few walnuts and add them in small pieces for an extra crunch. But they're not essential.

1 large garlic clove, peeled and crushed with a little salt

2 tablespoons tahini

³/4 cup plain yogurt

1 pound carrots, coarsely grated

2 tablespoons coarsely chopped cilantro or parsley

Sea salt and freshly ground black pepper

Put the crushed garlic in a large bowl. Stir the tahini well to prevent it from settling then add to the bowl with the yogurt, salt and pepper and mix thoroughly.

Add the carrots to the bowl and mix well. Stir in the cilantro.

Allow the salad to marinate for a few minutes for the flavors to develop before serving.

lima beans with chorizo

This is a great tapa found in most of Spain. There are mild and hot versions of chorizo—whichever you prefer, go for a quality one for the best result. Traditionally, the Spanish use dried beans which need to be soaked and cooked first. To moisten the beans, they add some of the cooking liquid. For a quicker version, I've used canned beans, but don't use the liquid; opt instead for a drier result—it's just as tasty.

1 small onion, chopped

1 garlic clove, chopped

1 tablespoon extra virgin olive oil

14 ounces canned lima beans

3¹/₂ ounces chorizo, hot or mild

3 tablespoons sherry

1 tablespoon flatleaf parsley, coarsely chopped (optional)

Sea salt and freshly ground black pepper

Heat a large lidded saucepan or sauté pan. Add the onion, garlic, and olive oil and gently cook, covered, for 5 minutes to soften.

Rinse and drain the lima beans and set aside.

Slice the chorizo into thin slices at an angle for an attractive look. Add the chorizo to the pan, and continue to gently cook for 5 minutes, uncovered, stirring occasionally.

Add the lima beans, season with salt and pepper, and add the sherry. Cover with the lid again and cook another 5 minutes.

Remove from the heat, check the seasoning, and put in a serving bowl scattered with the parsley, if using. Serve warm.

dukkah

SERVES 4–6
PREPARATION TIME 10 MINUTES COOKING TIME 10 MINUTES

This is a great Eygptian idea. Dukkah makes a delicious appetizer served with some yogurt and flatbread. Or try it with raw vegetables such as radishes, spring onions and tomatoes. It will keep for several weeks in an airtight container.

3¹/₂ ounces blanched hazelnuts

3¹/₂ ounces sesame seeds

2 heaped tablespoons coriander seeds

1 level tablespoon cumin seeds

1 heaped teaspoon sea salt

1 heaped teaspoon freshly ground black pepper

to serve

flatbread

extra virgin olive oil

thick drained yogurt or labnah

Preheat the oven to 350°F.

Place the nuts on separate trays and bake until they are golden brown. This takes about 5 minutes for the sesame seeds and 10 minutes for the hazelnuts. Set aside to cool.

Dry-roast first the coriander and then the cumin seeds in a skillet over medium heat for a few minutes until they start to very slightly color and give off a mild aroma. Be careful, as they burn easily.

Grind the spices using a mortar and pestle for best results (or a sturdy bowl and the end of a rolling pin is a good substitute). Work in batches if necessary. Transfer the spices to a bowl. Then grind half the sesame seeds and add the rest whole to the prepared spices. Coarsely grind all the hazelnuts so they keep some texture.

Mix the ingredients together and add the salt and pepper. Taste for correct seasoning. Place in a bowl, and put the olive oil and yogurt in two separate bowls.

To serve, dunk some flatbread first in the oil and then in the dukkah to make it stick and enjoy with a little yogurt or labnah.

soups and sauces

Soups and sauces feature in any cuisine and the Mediterraneans are particularly famous for their fish and seafood soups. Unfortunately, most of them take more than 30 minutes—if not half the day and using half the fish market! So preparing a quick fish soup was a challenge, but a pleasurable one.

It makes perfect sense to include typical Mediterranean sauces in this section as they're often served with a soup: an unctuous dollop dropped in the bowl at the last minute bringing a bright fresh taste, or a pungent fieriness, to the soup. Aioli (garlic mayonnaise) with saffron is easier to prepare than, say, the famous rouille that is always served with the equally famous bouillabaisse of France. Just as renowned in Spain is romesco sauce, a contribution from the proud Catalan people in the region around Barcelona.

Soups are a great way to start a meal, although they're often not seen as that adventurous a choice on a menu. Done well, hot or cold, they whet the appetite for what's to follow. Or they can become a hearty meal in themselves with some delicious bread served alongside.

There is something about soups that makes them great comfort food. Perhaps it's the fact that they simultaneously quench our thirst as well as satisfy our stomachs. For that reason, many often seem better served with a fork rather than a spoon.

clam and lardon soup

A dish from France where clams are called palourdes or praires. Bacon and fish are often paired together and this particular combination works really well, especially with the cream. It is very similar to New England-style chowder. Don't be tempted to add any salt to this recipe as the bacon and clams have more than enough themselves.

1 pound fresh clams

2 tablespoons extra virgin olive oil

1³/₄ ounces lardons or smoked bacon, cubed

1 small onion (3 heaped tablespoons, finely chopped)

2¹/₂ ounces potatoes

1 large garlic clove

1 heaped teaspoon thyme

Pinch of saffron

¹/₂ cup plus 1 extra tablespoon

dry white vermouth or white wine

¹/₂ cup heavy cream

Freshly ground black pepper

Place the clams in a large bowl or sink, cover with cold water and leave to soak.

Put the bacon and olive oil in a saucepan and cook over a medium heat. Chop the onion and add to the bacon. Peel the potatoes, chop into small cubes, and add to the onion mixture. Finely chop the garlic and strip the thyme leaves from the stems, coarsely chop and add to the bacon, stirring occasionally.

Soak the saffron in the tablespoon of vermouth and set aside.

While the onion is cooking, heat a high-sided lidded sauté pan or saucepan over a high heat. Remove the clams from the water individually, making sure that none are full of sand or grit and place in a colander. Add them to the hot pan, pour in the vermouth immediately and cover with a lid. Cook for 2 minutes, removing from the heat if bubbling too much. Drain over a bowl to catch the liquid.

Carefully pour the clam liquid into the onion and potato mixture, discarding any sediment (clams aren't as bad as mussels). Cover the pan and gently cook for 5 minutes.

Meanwhile, shell about half the clams (leave some intact, though: the shells look so good in the soup).

Make sure the potatoes are soft then add the cream and pepper to taste. Bring to a boil and add all the clams. Return to simmer, and serve immediately.

spinach, tarragon, and yogurt soup

This Turkish soup can be served hot or cold. It looks great served with a dollop of yogurt and a drizzle of peppery-tasting extra virgin olive oil. Instead of tarragon you can use mint or marjoram, but tarragon gives it a distinctive flavor. I used large leaf spinach for this recipe, because it gets puréed, so there's no need to worry about the stalks. Of course you can use ready-prepared spinach for extra speed.

4 tablespoons extra virgin olive oil

1 medium onion

2 garlic cloves

1³/4 pounds large leaf fresh spinach

4 heaped tablespoons chopped tarragon leaves

¹/2 whole nutmeg, freshly grated

3¹/2 cups chicken broth or water

1¹/4 cups Greek-style thick yogurt

2 heaped teaspoons cornstarch

Sea salt and freshly ground black pepper

to serve

Yogurt

Extra virgin olive oil

Heat the oil in a large saucepan. Chop the onion and garlic and gently cook for 5 minutes until the onion is soft.

Wash the spinach and drain. Break up the large leaves with your hands and add them to the pan. Keep stirring as they wilt, so that you can gradually add in all of the spinach. Strip the tarragon leaves from the stems, chop roughly, and add to the pan. Season with nutmeg, salt and pepper. Cook for a few minutes until all the leaves are wilted, then add the chicken broth and bring to a boil.

Blend the yogurt with the cornstarch. When the spinach stems are soft, add the yogurt mixture and stir well. Bring back to a boil, but don't overcook so the color stays bright green.

Remove from the heat and purée with a hand-held blender.

Serve the soup immediately or leave to chill. Add a spoonful of yogurt and a drizzle of olive oil to each bowl.

italian broccoli and broth soup

SERVES 4
PREPARATION TIME 15 MINUTES COOKING TIME 5 MINUTES

The Tuscans make this dish to celebrate the new season's extra virgin olive oil which is harvested in November. I find it a great winter soup to cope with all the excesses of the holiday season: physically and financially! The Italian name for it is Soupa di Povero—soup for the poor—as the ingredients are cheap and easy to come by in Italy. But as so often with Italian dishes, using the best-quality ingredients is what makes this a superb, simple dish. If you have homemade broth, do use this in preference to a stockcube or granules because the dried varieties just won't be the same.

4 thick slices country-style bread

1 large garlic clove, unpeeled

4 cups good-quality chicken broth

Dash of sherry or vermouth

14 ounces broccoli, cut into florets, or broccoli

of the season

1 ounce Parmesan, freshly grated

Drizzle of best-quality, single estate, new season extra virgin

olive oil

Sea salt and freshly ground black pepper

Toast or broil the bread and, while still hot, rub on both sides with the garlic. Halve each slice and place 2 halves in 4 warm shallow soup bowls.

Bring the chicken broth to a boil and add the sherry. Add the broccoli to the broth and cook for about 4 minutes—it needs to be cooked completely to bring out its flavor. Only pasta is "al dente" in Italy.

Place the broccoli on top of the bread, season with salt and pepper, and pour over the hot broth. Sprinkle with Parmesan and drizzle with olive oil and serve immediately.

squid, chickpea, and tomato soup

SERVES 4
PREPARATION TIME 5 MINUTES COOKING TIME 25 MINUTES

This soup would be served along the coasts of Morocco or Tunisia, making good use of the plentiful squid in the southern Mediterranean. I often use frozen squid for this recipe, as the freezing process tenderizes the flesh. Also, frozen squid are usually large and have the tentacles removed and cleaned, so they are easy to use.

3 tablespoons extra virgin olive oil

1 small onion

1 small fennel, or ½ large one

2 garlic cloves

½ large red chili

1 level tablespoon coriander seeds

1 level tablespoon cumin seeds

14 ounces prepared frozen squid, defrosted and drained

7 ounces tomatoes

14 ounces canned chickpeas, rinsed and drained

1³⁄₄ cups fish broth

2 tablespoons lemon juice

2 heaped tablespoons freshly chopped mint, cilantro, or dill

Sea salt and freshly ground black pepper

Gently heat the olive oil in a large, lidded saucepan. Chop the onion and add to the pan. Chop the fennel into small slices and add to the pan. Cover and cook for 10 minutes.

Slice the garlic and chop the chili. Grind the cilantro and cumin seeds in a pestle and mortar or spice grinder. As soon as you have prepared the spices, add the garlic, chili, and spices to the onion mixture, stirring well to prevent the onion mixture from burning and continue to cook with the lid on so that the onion cooks quickly.

Meanwhile, quarter the squid (if it's large) lengthwise and slice. Rinse and drain well on paper towels.

Uncover the pan, increase the heat to high and add the prepared squid, stirring frequently, so that it doesn't burn, and cook for 5 minutes. Cube the tomato and add with the chickpeas to the pan. Season with salt and pepper and cook for another 5 minutes, stirring frequently to prevent everything from sticking, but also to reduce the liquid. Add the broth and bring to a simmer. Cook for a further 5 minutes, then remove from the heat. Stir in the lemon juice and herbs and serve.

spanish fish soup with rice and saffron

SERVES 6 AS AN APPETIZER, OR 4 AS A MAIN COURSE
PREPARATION TIME 10 MINUTES COOKING TIME 20 MINUTES

I cannot do paella or risotto in under 30 minutes, but this hearty soup just squeezes into the time limit. It might take 35 minutes if using authentic Spanish paella rice, but I've found it works just as well with Basmati rice which cooks in less time. I had this soup looking out over the Med in a small fishing port in Spain and it seems one of the easiest fish soups I know—most take too long to prepare and cook.

2 pounds fresh clams

2¹/2 cups fish broth

7 ounces large raw headless shrimp (increase the weight if you buy them with heads on)

²/3 cup dry sherry or white wine

Large pinch of saffron

1 small onion, chopped

3 tablespoons extra virgin olive oil

2 garlic cloves

1 small red bell pepper

¹/2 large red chili, or ¹/2 teaspoon chili flakes

Heaped ¹/3 cup Basmati or long grain rice

12 ounces white firm-fleshed fish such as cod or monkfish

Flatleaf parsley, coarsely chopped, to serve

Put the clams in a large bowl or sink of cold water to soak. Remove the clams individually, checking to make sure none are full of sand or grit and place in a colander.

Pour the fish broth into a saucepan and bring to a gentle boil. Heat a large lidded sauté pan to medium-high ready for the clams.

Peel the shrimp, and set aside. Add the shrimp shells to the broth and gently simmer.

Increase the heat under the sauté pan to high and add the drained clams, making sure they don't crowd the pan. Pour over just ¹/3 cup of the sherry, cover the pan and cook quickly for 2 minutes. Drain over a bowl, reserving the liquid. Put the remaining sherry in a bowl with the saffron and leave to infuse.

Rinse the sauté pan, place back on the burner to dry, and turn the heat to low. Chop the onion and add with the olive oil to the pan. Cover and gently cook to soften the onion quickly. Meanwhile, chop the garlic and add, then seed and chop the pepper and add, finally chop and add the chili. Allow the onion to cook for 10 minutes in total to soften.

Add the rice and stir in to coat in the oil. Don't cook quickly as the rice should not brown.

Strain and measure the fish broth. You should have about 2 cups. Add the reserved clam juice, discarding any sediment, to make a total of 3¹/4 cups broth (add water if not enough). If you have too much fish broth then reserve some of it for another recipe, rather than the clam juice, as the juice of the clams is tastier. Add the measured broth and the sherry and saffron, rinsing the bowl to incorporate all the flavor of the saffron, to the rice and onions and bring to a boil.

Cut the fish into 1¹/2-inch cubes and the shrimp in half or thirds depending on size. Add the fish and shrimp to the broth, cover the pan and gently cook for 10–15 minutes, depending on the type of rice.

Meanwhile, remove the clams from their shell and set aside. Chop the parsley.

When the rice is just cooked, add the clams and parsley and serve immediately with warm crusty bread.

gazpacho

SERVES 4
PREPARATION TIME 25 MINUTES

There are many varieties of gazpacho, some white, some with lots of bread. This is my preferred version. It's perfect on a baking hot day—what you could call liquid lunch. The tarragon adds the extra taste dimension. Use good-quality tomatoes to make the soup really flavorsome. As this soup is served chilled I take vegetables straight from the fridge and that way the soup doesn't need to rest in the fridge before serving. Otherwise, you can add some ice cubes to speed up the process.

1 green bell pepper

1 red bell pepper

1 large cucumber

1 small red onion

1 pound ripe tasty tomatoes

3 tablespoons coarsely chopped tarragon leaves

2 large garlic cloves, chopped

3 tablespoons sherry vinegar

1 cup tomato juice

Sea salt and freshly ground black pepper

to serve

Croûtons (optional) or crusty bread

Finely diced vegetables (prepared from above ingredients)

Quarter the peppers, remove the seeds and white membrane. Finely dice 2 tablespoons of each color and set aside as a garnish, then coarsely chop the rest. Peel the cucumber, finely dice 2 tablespoons and set aside as a garnish, then coarsely chop the rest. Finely chop 1 tablespoon red onion and set aside as a garnish and coarsely chop the rest. Finely chop 2 tablespoons of tomatoes and set aside as a garnish and coarsely chop the rest.

Put the tarragon and garlic in a food processor with all the coarsely chopped vegetables. Blend everything to a purée. Season well with salt and pepper. Add the vinegar and tomato juice and serve, garnished with a little of the reserved vegetables in each bowl.

Traditionally this is served with croutons, cooked in olive oil and garlic. But warm crusty bread does just as well if you're in a hurry.

harissa sauce

SERVES 4–6
PREPARATION TIME 5 MINUTES COOKING TIME 25 MINUTES

Harissa is a hot pepper condiment and a traditional Moroccan relish. I find a lot of the bought versions too hot to handle. This recipe, given to me by a friend, works really well, as it's less fiery and has a nice homemade feel. Dry-roasting the spices gives a delicious smoky flavor.

3 red bell peppers

3 large red chilies

1 teaspoon coriander seeds

2 garlic cloves, peeled

1 heaped teaspoon tomato paste

1 teaspoon cumin seeds

4 tablespoons extra virgin olive oil

Preheat the broiler to hot. Broil the peppers, turning regularly, until the skin is completely blackened. Put in a plastic bag or in a lidded bowl and leave to cool.

Meanwhile, coarsely chop the chilies, removing the seeds if you want a milder sauce, and set aside.

Roast the cumin and coriander seeds in a hot dry skillet, then grind in a mortar and pestle or spice grinder.

Peel the skin from the cooled peppers, picking off all the black bits. Remove the stem but keep the seeds.

Put the peeled peppers, chilies, garlic, tomato paste, ground cumin, and coriander in a food processor with the olive oil and blitz to a smooth purée.

This keeps in the fridge for a couple of weeks in a jar with a thin film of olive oil on top to seal it.

romesco sauce

SERVES 4–6
PREPARATION TIME 5 MINUTES COOKING TIME 25 MINUTES

This is a Spanish recipe and there are many different versions of it. Traditionally, dried peppers (such as Noras) are used, but I have gone for the more readily available broiled peppers, which means the sauce is quick to prepare. If you can track down the dried version, soak them first in warm water. Romesco is delicious with grilled fish.

3 red bell peppers

4 tablespoons extra virgin olive oil

1 ounce whole or flaked almonds, blanched

1 ounce hazelnuts, skinned

2 garlic cloves

2 large red chilies, seeded (optional)

1 large tomato

1 heaped teaspoon coriander seeds, freshly ground

1 tablespoon sherry or red wine vinegar

Preheat the broiler to hot. Broil the peppers, turning regularly, until the skin is completely blackened. Put in a plastic bag or in a lidded bowl and leave to cool.

Meanwhile, heat a skillet and add 2 tablespoons of the olive oil. Toast the nuts until lightly browned.

Peel the skin from the cooled peppers, picking off all the black bits. Remove the seeds and stem.

Roughly chop the garlic, chilies, and tomato. Put the peeled peppers, garlic, chilies, tomato, nuts, and coriander in a food processor with the remaining olive oil and vinegar and blitz to a smooth purée.

This keeps in the fridge for a couple of weeks in a jar with a thin film of olive oil on top to seal it.

saffron aioli

SERVES 4–6
PREPARATION TIME 15 MINUTES

Aioli is a garlic mayonnaise. The experts say that a truly authentic mayonnaise should contain enough garlic to give you a brief headache when you eat it! Adding saffron makes it a lovely rich yellow color. This works very well with any fish recipe or as a dip for vegetables such as grilled asparagus (see page 92). Make it fresh each time, as it doesn't keep long.

2 large garlic cloves, smashed with a little salt

Juice ½ large lemon

1 large pinch of saffron threads, soaked in a little of the lemon juice

2 egg yolks

¾ cup plus 2 tablespoons extra virgin olive oil

Mix the garlic with the lemon juice and soaked saffron. Set aside.

Beat the egg yolks in a medium bowl and slowly pour in the olive oil, initially drop by drop, beating with a whisk, adding in a steady thin drizzle as the mixture thickens. If it becomes too thick, add a little extra lemon juice to thin it down. When all the oil has been added, mix in the garlic, lemon, and saffron mixture.

Cover with plastic wrap to prevent a skin from forming. Do not over-stir before serving as it might separate.

salsa verde

SERVES 6
PREPARATION TIME 10 MINUTES

This is an all-round sauce for meat, poultry, and fish dishes. Versions of it are found throughout Italy and neighboring islands.

2½ ounces anchovy fillets

1 level tablespoon capers

1 large garlic clove

Zest of 1 lemon

1 ounce fresh flatleaf parsley

½ ounce fresh mint

1 ounce fresh basil

1 tablespoon mild mustard

1 tablespoon good wine vinegar

4 tablespoons good-quality extra virgin olive oil

Sea salt and freshly ground black pepper

Rinse the anchovies and dry on paper towels. Put the anchovies, capers, garlic, and lemon zest in a food processor and finely chop. Pick the herb leaves off their stalks and add to the anchovy mixture. Mix only briefly with the anchovies to keep their bright color. Stir in the mustard, vinegar, oil, salt and pepper. Taste and correct the seasoning to your liking.

Tip: For best results make sure the herbs are as dry as possible before processing. The salsa can also be chopped by hand.

salads

One reason why the Mediterranean diet is so healthy is the abundance of salad, fruit, and vegetables consumed daily. There's a blurring between what is a salad and a vegetable dish. Some are simple affairs, others deliciously complex in flavors and textures. Not all salads are chilled—think of the French "salades tièdes": warm salads with softly wilting greens. Others, with a big protein component, might be a meal in themselves; these have relocated to other sections.

Salads are made for dressing and in the Mediterranean that means top-quality olive oil and vinegars or lemon juice, and fresh herbs for additional flavoring. A small bottle of really good extra virgin olive oil makes all the difference. (Keep it for dressing and drizzling as the flavor is impaired by cooking, and don't leave it by the stove to get hot nor allow it to become too cold.) Buy only in small quantities, though, because, once opened, it will slowly start to deteriorate and lose its freshness.

Olives are harvested in November, so look out for "new season oil." Stored well, good oil can last for 18 months, though I try to use new season oil once it gets to the shops. Buy olive oil for salads from a named grower. You can make the comparison with wine: consider it like drinking a great Bordeaux or Burgundy or "vin ordinaire". Oils vary hugely in flavor as well as quality. Taste the oils from the different Mediterranean countries to see which you like best. You also need to balance the oil with the right amount of acidity: too much and you will mask the quality and flavor of the oil. Here again, buy good-quality wine or sherry vinegar or use freshly squeezed lemon juice—it's worth it.

beet, green bean, and preserved lemon salad

SERVES 4
PREPARATION TIME 15 MINUTES COOKING TIME 3 MINUTES

This is a stunning yet incredibly easy dish. I was served it along with other mezze when visiting friends in Morocco. Use as part of a selection of mezze, serve as a starter or as a great accompaniment to fish. If you can't find preserved lemons, then substitute the zest of 1 large lemon.

8 ounces green beans

2 large heads beets (1 pound), cooked

1 slice (¼ lemon) preserved lemon or zest of 1 lemon

1 packet or small bunch mint or parsley, leaves stemmed and coarsely chopped

4 tablespoons extra virgin olive oil to drizzle

Sea salt and freshly ground black pepper

Trim the beans while you bring a saucepan of water to a boil. Blanch the beans for about 3 minutes. Drain and refresh the beans under cold water then set aside to dry.

Peel and slice the beet into thin disks. Place them neatly overlapping on a flat dish. Briefly rinse the lemon and remove the white membrane. Finely chop or slice the skin of the lemon.

Scatter the beans in the middle of the beets and sprinkle over the preserved lemon and chopped mint. Drizzle with olive oil and season the salad with salt and pepper.

Serve with Moroccan flatbread or pita bread.

cucumber salad with pomegranates and mint

SERVES 4
PREPARATION TIME 20 MINUTES

Cucumbers appear in salads throughout the Mediterranean region as they are so refreshing in the heat, while pomegranates are a regular feature in Middle Eastern recipes. This is one of my favorites, as it's so unusual, and the color contrast of the pale green cucumber and the pink pomegranate looks amazing. Serve with other mezze or seasoned yogurt and warm flatbread. Mediterranean cucumbers are very different from our hot-house varieties. They have little water and therefore stay much crunchier when mixed with salt and other ingredients.

1 large cucumber

1 pomegranate

1 large garlic clove

2 scallions

2 heaped tablespoons mint leaves, plus sprigs to garnish

2 tablespoons lime juice

Sea salt and freshly ground black pepper

Peel the cucumber, slice thinly at an attractive angle and place in a bowl.

Cut the pomegranate into quarters and turn out the skin to make it easier to remove the seeds. Discard any yellow pith that comes away as well. You need about 6 tablespoons of the seeds. Place them in the bowl with the cucumber.

Smash the garlic with salt in a mortar and pestle or with a knife and finely chop the scallions and mint. Add all these ingredients and the lime juice to the bowl and season with salt and pepper. Mix well and leave to marinate a little if you have time before serving.

eggplant, tomato, and mint salad

SERVES 6
PREPARATION TIME 10 MINUTES COOKING TIME 15 MINUTES

Eggplant is widely grown around the Mediterranean and regularly features in salads and side dishes: this one is another delicious recipe from Turkey.

1 pound eggplant, trimmed and cut into slices ½ inch thick

about 1 cup extra virgin olive oil

3½ ounces vine-grown or any flavorsome tomatoes

3 medium scallions (green and white parts), trimmed

1 garlic clove

2 tablespoons red wine vinegar or lemon juice

2 heaped tablespoons coarsely chopped mint, plus

sprigs to garnish

Sea salt and freshly ground black pepper

Heat a large skillet or sauté pan with about half the oil over a medium-high heat while you slice the eggplant. (You need to be generous with the oil so that the eggplant fries, not burns, in the pan.) Add just enough slices to cover the bottom of the pan and cook on both sides for about 4 minutes until golden brown and soft. Remove from the pan and drain on paper towels. Add more oil as necessary and repeat until all the eggplant is cooked.

Meanwhile, quarter or chop the tomatoes (depending on size) and finely chop the scallions. Place in a bowl. Smash the garlic with salt in a mortar and pestle or with a knife and mix with the tomato, scallions, and vinegar. Season the mixture with pepper and a little salt (depending on how much you used with the garlic).

Once the eggplant slices have drained, cut in half and gently combine with the tomato mixture. Add the mint and, if time, leave to marinate to enhance the flavor.

Serve with other mezze or warm pita bread.

broiled eggplant with coriander and chili

SERVES 2
PREPARATION TIME 10 MINUTES COOKING TIME 20 MINUTES

Another recipe for eggplant that just meets the 30-minute rule! Make sure they are properly cooked, rather than simply go by the color, as raw eggplant tastes horrible. Cook all the eggplant, placing them one on top of the other once cooked. This helps them to steam a little and soften. Don't slice them thinly, or they will burn before they have chance to cook.

1 large (1 pound) eggplant, trimmed and cut into slices ½ inch thick

1 heaped teaspoon coriander seeds

1 garlic clove

½ large fresh chili (you need 2 teaspoons, finely chopped)

2 heaped tablespoons coarsely chopped parsley or mint

4 tablespoons good-quality extra virgin olive oil

2 tablespoons red wine vinegar or lemon juice

Sea salt and freshly ground black pepper

Preheat a dry griddle on the burner while you slice the eggplant. Cover the griddle with slices and cook over a medium-high heat for about 10 minutes, turning half way through cooking until the eggplant is soft and cooked.

Meanwhile, toast the coriander seeds in a small dry skillet, until lightly golden and mildly aromatic—this enhances the flavor. Grind in a mortar and pestle or spice grinder.

Smash the garlic with about 1 teaspoon salt in a mortar and pestle or with a knife. Finely chop the chili, omitting the seeds if you want less heat, and coarsely chop the mint. Mix together the crushed garlic, coriander, chili, olive oil, vinegar, parsley, and some black pepper in a large bowl to make a marinade.

Add the eggplant, stirring gently to avoid breaking up the slices, and serve. It's good with arugula salad or warm flatbread.

SALADS

51

bread salad
(fattoush)

SERVES 4
PREPARATION TIME 20 MINUTES COOKING TIME 5 MINUTES

Fattoush is a traditional Lebanese salad which utilizes leftover bread that soaks up the delicious dressing. It can include different vegetables according to what is available. What makes it a Lebanese fattoush is the inclusion of sumac, the sour fruity spice that is identified with Lebanese cooking, and the toasted pita bread. I describe it as the equivalent of an Italian panzanella salad.

3 large pita bread

1 bunch of radishes (5 ounces), trimmed

3½ ounces tomatoes

3 scallions, trimmed

½ cucumber, peeled, halved lengthwise and seeded

1 small green bell pepper

5 ounces cauliflower

1 large garlic clove

Juice of 1 lemon (4 tablespoons)

⅔ cup extra virgin olive oil

1 heaped tablespoon sumac

1 small head romaine lettuce, outer leaves removed

3 heaped tablespoons coarsely chopped flatleaf parsley

3 heaped tablespoons coarsely chopped mint

1 ounce arugula

Sea salt and freshly ground black pepper

Preheat the oven to 400°F.

Open up the pita bread and spread out on a baking sheet without overlapping so that they dry out evenly. Toast in the oven for about 5–10 minutes until lightly browned and crisp. Remove, allow to cool, then break the bread into small pieces.

Meanwhile, thinly slice the radishes, chop the tomatoes, scallions, cucumber, and pepper into small pieces and the cauliflower into florets. Put everything into a serving bowl.

Smash the garlic with salt in a mortar and pestle or with a knife. Mix the garlic with the lemon juice, olive oil, pepper, and sumac. Add the dressing to the vegetables and mix well.

Chop the herbs and lettuce and add to the bowl with the bread, and mix to combine.

Taste and adjust the seasoning as necessary and serve.

leeks with caper, parsley, and anchovy sauce

SERVES 4
PREPARATION TIME 10 MINUTES COOKING TIME 15 MINUTES

Salted anchovies are used in abundance in Mediterranean cooking, more as a salty seasoning than a piece of fish, but you can omit them from this recipe if you wish.

6 large leeks (about 1³/₄ pounds trimmed weight)

6 anchovies, finely chopped

1 large garlic clove

2 tablespoons coarsely chopped flatleaf parsley

Zest of 1 lemon and 3 tablespoons juice

1 tablespoon capers

9 tablespoons extra virgin olive oil

Sea salt and freshly ground black pepper

Bring a saucepan of salted water to a boil. Cut through the green part of the leeks to the center of the stem (but keep them whole) to make it easier to wash away any mud. Wash thoroughly and add to the pan of boiling water, immersing completely as they soften, and cook for about 15 minutes until soft.

Meanwhile, rinse the anchovies and dry on paper towels. Smash the garlic with a little salt, chop the anchovies and parsley, zest and juice the lemon, and rinse and chop the capers. Transfer all the prepared ingredients to a small bowl. Add the olive oil, season with salt and pepper, mix well, and set aside.

When the leeks are cooked, drain in a large colander, being careful they don't disintegrate too much. Press with a plate that fits into the colander or use a large spoon to squeeze out any water. Place several sheets of paper towels in a shallow rectangular dish, put the leeks on top and wrap briefly to absorb any remaining water. Arrange the leeks in the dish, pour over the caper mixture and leave to marinate for a few minutes or longer. Serve warm or at room temperature.

borlotti and green bean salad

SERVES 4–6
PREPARATION TIME 15 MINUTES COOKING TIME 5 MINUTES

Italians often combine pulses with legumes. I use borlotti beans, but cannellini beans work just as well. Fresh borlotti beans need to be cooked first, but they are far superior to the canned version and take less time to cook than dried. If you don't eat meat, anchovy fillets are a good substitute for the pancetta—add them to warm through with the beans. Try this salad with some meaty fish such as turbot or monkfish, or serve as a starter with some arugula.

7 ounces green beans, trimmed

3¹/₂ ounces smoked pancetta or bacon, diced

2 garlic cloves

1 heaped tablespoon finely chopped sage or rosemary

3 tablespoons good-quality extra virgin olive oil (use salad variety for the dressing)

28 ounces (2 cans) canned borlotti beans, rinsed and drained, or 14 ounces fresh beans, cooked

10 ounces tomatoes (use cherry tomatoes out of season)

2 tablespoons good-quality red wine vinegar

Trim the beans while you bring a saucepan of water to a boil. Cook the green beans for about 3 minutes. Drain well and cut in half. Set aside.

Dice the pancetta if necessary. Finely chop the garlic and sage. Heat 1 tablespoon of the oil in a skillet and cook the pancetta on a medium-high heat until just golden brown. Push to the sides and tilt the oil back into the middle of the pan. Cook the garlic and sage until just light brown, then add the borlotti beans and mix briefly. Remove from the heat.

Cut the tomatoes into small chunks and place in a large bowl. Add the drained green beans and borlotti beans. Pour over the remaining 2 tablespoons of oil and the wine vinegar. Mix to combine and serve.

deep-fried zucchini salad with mint and chili

SERVES 2–4
PREPARATION TIME 15 MINUTES COOKING TIME 15 MINUTES

This is delicious with simply broiled fish. The dish might seem like a labor of love but it's worth it if you're only cooking for up to four people. I can easily eat half this amount, but it can stretch to four if you want. Use a red chili, as the color contrasts well with the green of the zucchini.

2½ pounds zucchini, trimmed

1 cup extra virgin olive oil

½ large red chili, finely chopped

1 heaped tablespoon mint leaves, coarsely chopped or torn

1 tablespoon good red wine vinegar

Sea salt

Preheat a large skillet to medium-hot and line a large plate or serving dish with paper towels.

Wash, dry, and very thinly slice the zucchini. (You can use a food processor with a slicer attachment or a mandolin. But if you slice and cook at the same time, you can do it perfectly easily by hand within the time.)

After you have sliced one zucchini, add the oil to the skillet and individually place the slices in the pan, just enough to cover the bottom. This prevents them from sticking together.

Cook the zucchini for about 1 minute or until the underside is just golden brown. Using a slotted spoon, turn the slices over and cook on the second side until just golden brown. Remove with the slotted spoon, draining as much of the oil as possible back into the pan and place the slices on the paper towels.

While the first zucchini cooks, thinly slice the remaining ones, cooking and cutting in batches until they are all cooked and drained. Remove the paper towels and spread out the zucchini on the plate. Finely chop the chilli and chop or tear the mint. Drizzle over the vinegar, season well with salt, and carefully mix. Scatter over the chili and mint and serve.

fennel and orange salad

SERVES 4–6
PREPARATION TIME 15–20 MINUTES

Sicilians use their abundance of oranges in salads as well as sweets. Blood oranges when in season make a great color contrast, but ordinary ones taste just as good. The bright pinkish-red seeds of fresh pomegranates are an optional extra used to decorate dishes—an Arabian influence—if you can't get blood oranges. This is a very simple but refreshing salad, ideal for the winter months and a great accompaniment to oily rich foods. The trick with this salad is to make sure the fennel is sliced finely.

3 large fennel bulbs, trimmed

1 large orange, juiced (about 4 tablespoons of juice)

8 tablespoons extra virgin olive oil

1 ounce arugula or a bunch of watercress

Handful of dill sprigs

2–3 oranges (blood oranges in season)

seeds from 1 ripe pomegranate (optional)

Sea salt and freshly ground black pepper

Cut the fennel bulbs in half from the top to the bottom and remove and discard the tough triangular-shaped heart. Finely slice the fennel and transfer to a bowl, adding the orange juice and olive oil immediately to prevent the fennel from discoloring. Season with salt and pepper.

Peel the oranges, removing all the inner white pith, then slice finely.

Put the arugula on a serving plate and top with the marinated fennel. Sprinkle with the dill and top with the orange slices. Scatter with pomegranate seeds, if using, and serve immediately.

Tip: Avoid using a carbon steel knife when preparing the fennel to keep the slices as white as possible.

marinated cauliflower and carrot with cumin and cardamom

SERVES 4

PREPARATION TIME 15 MINUTES   COOKING TIME 5–10 MINUTES

Many Mediterranean recipes are based on cooked vegetables marinated in lemon and oil. The Italians will use basil and capers, the Syrians and Lebanese will add spices such as cumin or herbs such as dill. When boiling the vegetables you can add a pinch of turmeric if you wish, to make the cauliflower turn a nice yellow color. You may find you have some marinade left over. This can always be mopped up with bread, or used again to marinate more vegetables!

8 ounces cauliflower florets

10 ounces carrots

1 garlic clove, smashed with salt

1 heaped tablespoon cumin

8 whole cardamom pods, split

3 tablespoons lemon juice

6 tablespoons extra virgin olive oil

1 heaped tablespoon fresh dill leaves

1 teaspoon fresh or dried red chili, chopped

Sea salt

Bring a saucepan of salted water to a boil.

Cut the cauliflower into smallish florets. Peel and thickly slice the carrots at an angle for attractive results. Cook the vegetables for 5–10 minutes, depending on whether you prefer your vegetables soft or crunchy. Drain well.

Meanwhile, smash the garlic with salt in a mortar and pestle or with a knife. Add the cumin and coarsely crush, then add the cardamom and open up the pods a little to release the flavor of the seeds. Add the lemon juice and oil and mix briefly. Put this mixture into a bowl. Chop the dill and chili and add to the other spices.

Add the drained vegetables while still hot and mix well, seasoning with more salt if need be.

Leave to marinate for at least 10 minutes before serving, or serve at room temperature.

SALADS

pasta, rice, and legumes

Rice is probably the most universal starch of the region but pasta and legumes are other staples. These three ingredients make meals that are sustaining and satisfying. They crop up everywhere, in soups, salads, and main courses. They are essential pantry items in the Mediterranean kitchen.

While we might view pasta as purely Italian, it is now found throughout the Mediterranean—if not the world—and many nations have adapted it, including the French, or even the Turks with their yogurt sauces over tortellini shapes (mantal ravioli). On the Mediterranean's southern shores, though, the staple of the countries of the Middle East and North Africa is cracked wheat. It goes in salads, stuffings and is served steamed as an accompaniment to meat and fish. Countries such as Syria and Lebanon also include a lot of Basmati rice in their recipes which is quicker to cook than the traditional varieties that are grown in the region. The number of different types of rice is fascinating: each grain type is subtly different and therefore makes entirely different dishes. It is hard to include some of the more elaborate Mediterranean recipes, such as risottos, paellas, or slow-cooked pilaffs, because of the time it takes to cook them, unless the rice is simply boiled. So Basmati is probably the quickest rice to use in these recipes.

There are also many different legumes, too, equally delicious and easily made into sophisticated dishes we might not think of. Legumes might have got a bad press in the 70s, yet they have been part of the Mediterranean diet for centuries. The legume dishes work well with fish, vegetables, or meat and many of the recipes are complete meals in themselves.

pasta with clams

SERVES 4
PREPARATION TIME 15 MINUTES COOKING TIME 15 MINUTES

This is a simple fish pasta, served in coastal towns throughout Italy, made with fresh clams (you'll see it as "pasta alla vongole" on menus). There's no need to add any extra salt apart from the pasta cooking water—clams are salty enough. You need to assemble your guests before you start to cook this dish because it is at its best eaten right away. Don't serve with cheese as this pasta contains chili and fish: it's just not done!

2 pounds clams, cleaned and drained

2 large garlic cloves

1 large red chili

1 small bunch flatleaf parsley

10 ounces linguine

¼ cup plus 1 tablespoon dry white vermouth or white wine

⅓ cup extra virgin olive oil

Place the clams in a large bowl or sink and cover with cold water and leave to soak. Leave for a few minutes, then remove the clams individually to make sure none are full of sand or grit, and place in a colander. Drain well.

Finely chop the garlic and chili, removing the seeds if you prefer less heat, and coarsely chop the parsley. Set aside.

Bring a large saucepan of well-salted water to a boil for the pasta. Heat a high-sided lidded sauté pan or saucepan for the clams.

Have all the ingredients ready then add the pasta to the boiling water, mixing well to coat each strand with water so they don't stick together.

Transfer the clams to the hot sauté pan, add the vermouth and cover with a lid. Cook for about 1–2 minutes until all the clams have opened. Drain over a bowl to catch the liquid.

Add the oil to the sauté pan and cook the garlic and chili briefly, then add the parsley and the clam liquid, discarding any sediment. Cook the liquid for a few minutes to concentrate the flavors.

Check to make sure the pasta is al dente, then drain well and add to the clam liquid. At the last minute, add the clams, mixing the pasta off the heat. Serve immediately, dividing first the pasta between bowls and then the clams for easiest results. Pour any remaining juices over each serving.

E. Efron de 25 épreuves ... par l'Estampe ... M. Lurs

Mary Cassatt

NATIONAL MUSEUM *of* WOMEN *in the* ARTS

Mary Cassatt (American, 1844–1926)

Maternal Caress, c. 1890–1891
Color print with drypoint and soft-ground etching, 14 1/2 x 10 9/16 in.
Gift of John and Linda Comstock in loving memory of Abigail Pearson Van Vleck

syrian rice with spinach and dates

SERVES 4-6
PREPARATION TIME 5 MINUTES COOKING TIME 25 MINUTES

The Middle Eastern countries that fringe the southern shores of the Mediterranean use a lot of Basmati rice, and most of it is slow cooked with meat—mainly lamb. This dish is an adaptation using all the appropriate ingredients except the lamb to speed up the time.

4 tablespoons extra virgin olive oil

1 medium onion

2 garlic cloves

2 cups chicken or lamb broth

Pinch of saffron

1 cup Basmati rice

4½ ounces pitted dates

1 level teaspoon ground cinnamon

¼ teaspoon freshly grated nutmeg

8 ounces cleaned and trimmed baby spinach

Sea salt and freshly ground black pepper

Heat a lidded sauté pan or saucepan over a medium heat and add the olive oil. Chop the onion and cook for 5 minutes. Chop the garlic and add to the pan.

Gently warm the chicken broth with the saffron to infuse.

Rinse the rice in cold water, changing the water several times, to remove as much of the starch as possible. Leave in the final rinsing water until ready to use.

Coarsely chop the dates. Add the spices to the onion mixture along with the dates and about half the spinach. Cook over a medium-high heat, stirring until wilted, then add the rest of the spinach when there is room for it. Season with salt and pepper.

When all the spinach is just wilted, add the drained rice. Mix well to incorporate and add the warm broth. Mix again, check for seasoning and cover with a lid. Cook gently for 10–15 minutes, stirring only briefly if it's cooking too quickly to prevent it from burning. (The more you stir, the more glutinous the rice.)

Remove the rice from the heat once it is just cooked and the broth has evaporated. Set the pan aside for 5 minutes or longer, still covered, to infuse the flavors and allow the rice to absorb all the liquid. Serve immediately.

shrimp, white bean, and dill salad

SERVES 4
PREPARATION TIME 20 MINUTES COOKING TIME 5 MINUTES

This salad is from Morocco, a country colonized by France. Most Moroccans speak French and the influence of French cooking is still apparent. Here, arugula is used like a herb, more for its peppery flavor than as a decorative bed of leaves for other ingredients. The shrimp can be smaller or larger—go with whatever is fresh and available but do buy raw ones. Check the amount carefully: raw shrimp are often sold frozen or packed with ice, thus 2 pounds of frozen shrimp when defrosted and drained, weigh 1 pound! I prefer to buy shrimp with the shell on. It takes only about 10 minutes to remove the shells for this recipe and I keep them in the freezer to add sweetness and improve the flavor when I'm making fish broth. But if you're in a real hurry you can buy small peeled shrimp and omit this task.

14 ounces canned white beans

1 pound medium to large raw headless shrimp

3½ ounces large tomato

2½ ounces arugula

½ large lemon (you need 3 tablespoons lemon juice)

1 large garlic clove

1–2 teaspoons coarsely ground cumin seeds

(depending on freshness)

½ large mild red chili

3 tablespoons coarsely chopped dill, leaves only

5 tablespoons extra virgin olive oil

Rinse and drain the beans well. Set aside.

Rinse and drain the shrimp well. Peel them, reserving or freezing the shells for another time, and place the shrimp on paper towels to absorb any remaining water. Set aside.

Cut the tomato into chunks and place in a large salad bowl. Coarsely chop the arugula and add to the tomatoes.

Gently heat a large skillet. Coarsely grind the cumin in a mortar and pestle or spice grinder. Juice the lemon. Finely chop the garlic, chili, and dill. Set aside.

Turn up the heat under the skillet to high and add 2 tablespoons of the oil to the hot pan. Add enough shrimp to cover the bottom of the pan and cook them for 1 minute. (Cook in batches if there are too many shrimp to fit in the pan, as they should be cooked quickly and fiercely to retain their juices and prevent them from drying out.) Quickly turn over the shrimp, cook for 1 minute then push a little to the side so you can fit the cumin, garlic, and chili into the pan. Add 1 more tablespoon of oil on top of the spices so they get a chance to quickly fry in oil, and not burn on the bottom of the pan. Cook briefly until the garlic starts to lightly brown, add the white beans and quickly add the lemon juice and dill. Remove from the heat, season with salt and pepper, and mix briefly.

Pour over the tomatoes and arugula in the bowl, add 2 more tablespoons of extra virgin olive oil to the salad and serve warm or marinated at room temperature. If you wish to prepare in advance, you might want to add the arugula when the shrimp are cool.

Tip: To devein shrimp quickly and easily, start peeling from the top of the body and carefully remove the tail. That way the dark vein often comes away easily with it.

bulgar wheat with chickpeas, pinenuts, and currants

SERVES 4
PREPARATION TIME 5 MINUTES COOKING TIME 20 MINUTES

The combination of cracked wheat (known as bulgar, burghul, or burghal, depending on where you are) and chickpeas is very common in Turkey, Syria, and the Lebanon. Mixing in pinenuts, currants, and spices makes it a little more special and sweeter. This is a good substitute for potatoes to serve as a side dish with meat or fish.

2 tablespoons extra virgin olive oil

1 small onion

1 garlic clove

1 ounce pinenuts

14 ounces canned chickpeas, rinsed and drained

1 ounce currants

1 level teaspoon allspice

2 heaped tablespoons coarsely chopped flatleaf parsley

3/4 cup bulgar wheat, fine or coarse

Sea salt and freshly ground black pepper

Heat a lidded sauté pan or saucepan over a medium heat and add the oil. Chop the onion and garlic. Cook the onion, garlic, and pinenuts for about 10 minutes until the onion is soft and translucent and the pinenuts are very lightly browned.

Rinse the chickpeas well and drain.

When the onions are soft, add the chickpeas, currants, and spices and stir to coat them in oil for a few minutes. Add the bulgar wheat, salt and pepper and mix well. Stir in 1 cup hot water, mix well, then cover the pan and cook gently for about 10 minutes. Check periodically to ensure the bottom doesn't stick. If the liquid has evaporated and the mixture is sticking to the bottom of the pan, leave for 1 minute to soften and then stir well. Add the parsley and serve.

rice, lentils, and spices

SERVES 4
PREPARATION TIME 5 MINUTES COOKING TIME 25 MINUTES

This is a delicious Middle Eastern dish called Mujadarra. It works well with simple broiled meats and fish. Gale at the London deli Baker and Spice gave me this version and it's one of the most moreish recipes I know.

1/2 cup Puy lentils or black lentils

1/2 cup Basmati rice

4 tablespoons olive oil

1/2 teaspoon ground cinnamon

1/2 teaspoon ground ginger

1/2 teaspoon turmeric

1/2 teaspoon ground allspice

2 tablespoons butter

2 medium onions, halved and thinly sliced

Sea salt and freshly ground black pepper

Rinse the lentils in cold water and leave to soak until ready to use. Briefly rinse the rice in cold water to remove as much starch as possible. Drain the lentils and rice thoroughly before proceeding.

Gently heat 2 tablespoons of the oil in a saucepan, add the spices, stir briefly, then add the lentils and rice and mix well. Add the butter and 1 2/3 cups water to the pan, cover with a lid, and bring to a boil. Stir the butter into the lentils and rice, lower the heat to a gentle simmer, cover the pan and gently cook the mixture for 25 minutes.

Meanwhile, halve and thinly slice the onions. Put the remaining oil in a skillet over a medium-high heat and cook the onions, stirring frequently, until brown and caramelized. Season with salt and pepper.

Once the rice is cooked, set the pan aside for 5 minutes, still covered, to steam. When the onions are ready, stir them into the rice. Serve either hot or at room temperature.

spinach and chickpea stew

SERVES 4
PREPARATION TIME 10 MINUTES COOKING TIME 20 MINUTES

Egyptians love to use chickpeas and they combine successfully with tomatoes—the acidity often softens them more. I have used baby spinach (ready washed) for quickest results.

2 tablespoons sunflower oil

1 medium onion, quartered and finely sliced

1 heaped tablespoon ground cumin seeds (or use ground)

1 heaped tablespoon ground coriander seeds

1/2 large red chili, finely chopped, or 1 teaspoon

chili flakes

1 large garlic clove, finely chopped

14 ounces canned chopped tomatoes

14 ounces canned chickpeas

5 ounces prepared baby spinach

Sea salt and freshly ground black pepper

to serve

Thick drained yogurt seasoned with 1 tablespoon

chopped cilantro

Warm Middle Eastern flatbread

Pour the oil into a lidded medium saucepan and gently cook the onion for about 10 minutes, covered, stirring periodically to prevent burning. Meanwhile, grind the spices. Add the cumin, coriander, chili, and garlic and cook for a minute longer, stirring periodically.

Add the tomatoes and cook another 10 minutes until reduced, stirring occasionally to prevent it from sticking to the bottom.

Rinse the chickpeas well then drain. Add the chickpeas and 1/2 cup water to the pan once the tomatoes have reduced. Season with salt and pepper and cook gently for a few minutes.

Add the spinach, stirring, until it wilts into the chickpea mixture, adding a dash of water if the tomatoes have reduced too much.

Remove from the heat and leave to rest a few minutes. Serve warm with a dollop of seasoned yogurt and some warm flatbread.

squid ink pasta sauce

SERVES 4 AS AN APPETIZER OR MEDIUM-SIZE MAIN COURSE
PREPARATION TIME 15 MINUTES COOKING TIME 15 MINUTES

This dish is most impressive as the pasta turns black when mixed with the sauce. The squid ink shouldn't stain your hands or apron, once washed. You can buy packets of ink from a fishmonger which is easier than attempting to extract it yourself! The packets last for some time in the fridge and can be frozen. If you can get your fishmonger to clean the squid for you, so much the better, but I include instructions anyway.

14 ounces squid (large frozen carcasses work well)

2 tablespoons extra virgin olive oil

1 small onion

1 small fennel bulb

1 large garlic clove

1 teaspoon finely chopped chili (optional)

4 small packets squid ink

½ cup dry white wine or vermouth

12½ ounces linguine or spaghetti

2 heaped tablespoons coarsely chopped flatleaf parsley

Sea salt and freshly ground black pepper

Heat a large lidded sauté or saucepan pan to medium-high or, if you are cleaning the squid yourself, heat the pan when you are slicing the squid.

To clean the squid, pull the heads and tentacles from the bodies with any innards. Remove the transparent vertebrae and cut down the ridge that remains, so that the squid is completely flat on a chopping board. Scrape away any sand and innards from the middle. Cut the heads off below the eyes and discard, leaving just the tentacles. Rinse the squid thoroughly in cold water, checking the suckers on the tentacles in particular have any lingering sand removed. Finely slice the tentacles and quarter the carcasses. Leave to drain well on paper towels.

Add the olive oil to the heated pan and add the prepared squid. Cook quickly, stirring occasionally to prevent the pieces from burning, so that their moisture is sealed in.

Bring a large saucepan of well-salted hot water to a boil.

While the squid is cooking, chop the onion and add to the pan. Quarter the fennel, remove and discard the tough triangular heart, and finely chop the rest. Add to the pan. Slice the garlic and add that, along with the chili, if using. Season with salt and pepper and cook gently.

Cut open the packets of squid ink, squeeze the ink into a bowl and mix in the vermouth.

When the onion and fennel are soft, add the vermouth and squid ink, bring to a gentle simmer, cover with a lid and cook slowly for about 10 minutes. (If necessary, you can add some of the pasta cooking water to ensure there is enough sauce to cover the pasta.)

While the sauce is cooking, cook the pasta, timing it carefully to coincide with the sauce being ready. Most good-quality dried pasta takes between 8 and 10 minutes—check the packet instructions. Cook the pasta, mixing well at the beginning, so the strands don't stick together. There's no need to add oil if the pasta is well mixed at the start.

Meanwhile, coarsely chop the parsley.

Drain the pasta when it is just al dente. Check the sauce to ensure that it is sufficiently liquid to cover the pasta and that the squid is tender. Mix the pasta into the sauce off the heat, sprinkle with parsley and serve immediately.

Tip: The sauce can be prepared in advance and kept in the fridge. Reheat it gently before adding the cooked pasta and you may need to dilute it with a little of the pasta cooking water.

pasta with anchovies, bell peppers, and pangritata

SERVES 4
PREPARATION TIME 15 MINUTES   COOKING TIME 15 MINUTES

If using fish or chilies in a pasta sauce, the Italians never serve Parmesan, so don't be tempted to offer any. Pangritata is the Italian name for toasted breadcrumbs cooked in oil and garlic. They add a crispy crunch to the pasta sauce and are often served with an oil-based pepper sauce instead of Parmesan. If you are broiling your own bell peppers keep them whole, which helps to soften them (see page 42), and putting them in a plastic bag until cool enough to handle makes them easier to peel. But when time is short, there are some very good jars of ready broiled bell peppers available now.

2 large garlic cloves

7 tablespoons extra virgin olive oil

1³/2 ounces (about 5 heaped tablespoons)
coarse fresh breadcrumbs

2 broiled red bell peppers

2 broiled yellow bell peppers

3¹/2 ounces salted anchovies

¹/2–1 large red chili

4 heaped tablespoons coarsely chopped flatleaf parsley

Sea salt and freshly ground black pepper

12–14 ounces penne

Smash the garlic with a little salt using a knife or a mortar and pestle. Pour 3 tablespoons of olive oil into a skillet and mix in the garlic. Add the breadcrumbs, mix well and cook gently, stirring continuously as they burn very easily. When they are just golden brown, remove from heat, season with salt and place in a bowl, ready for serving. This can be prepared in advance.

Bring a saucepan of well-salted water to a boil. Cut the peppers into thin strips and place in a bowl. Rinse the anchovies, dry on paper towels, then finely chop them and the chili. Coarsely chop the parsley and add everything to the peppers with the remaining 4 tablespoons of oil. Check the seasoning. This stage can be prepared in advance, too.

Add the pasta to the boiling water, mixing well to prevent any strands from sticking together, and cook until al dente. Drain, reserving a cup of water to loosen the pasta sauce. Return the pasta to the saucepan, off the heat. Add the anchovy sauce, mix well adding a little pasta water if necessary.

Serve immediately with the pangritata sprinkled on top.

lentil salad with lardons and walnuts

SERVES 4
PREPARATION TIME 5 MINUTES COOKING TIME 20–25 MINUTES

Puy lentils, which come from the Auvergne region of France, are the best to use for this recipe as they keep their shape, and don't require pre-soaking. This dish is a delicious combination of flavors and textures.

1 cup Puy lentils

2 garlic cloves, one whole, one chopped

3 tablespoons extra virgin olive oil plus extra for cooking and serving

3½ ounces smoked lardons, bacon or pancetta, cubed

1 medium onion

1¾ ounces walnut pieces

1 tablespoon thyme leaves, stemmed and coarsely chopped

Sea salt and freshly ground black pepper

Place the lentils in a saucepan and cover generously with hot water. Add the whole garlic clove and a dash of oil. Cover with a lid and bring to a boil. Once boiling, lower the heat to a simmer and cook for 20 minutes, until they are just soft, but not mushy.

Meanwhile, pour 3 tablespoons of oil into a skillet and cook the bacon on high until slightly crispy. While it cooks, quarter the onion then slice. Add the onion to the bacon, lower the heat, and add the walnuts, chopped garlic, and thyme and season with salt and pepper. Cook the onion slowly for about 20 minutes, stirring occasionally.

When the lentils are cooked, drain well and add to the onion mixture. Remove from the heat and serve either hot or cold.

pasta with zucchini, bottarga, and lemon zest

SERVES 4 AS A MAIN COURSE
PREPARATION TIME 10 MINUTES   COOKING TIME 15 MINUTES

This is a great Sicilian recipe using bottarga—dried mullet or tuna roe—see page 8. It has a very subtle flavor; think in terms of taramasalata. If you can't find bottarga, substitute ricotta. Mint adds a zing to the sauce but basil is just as good. The lemon zest keeps the flavor fresh. Traditionally pasta with bottarga doesn't include zucchini, but the flavor works well.

3 large zucchini (about 1½ pounds), washed

3 tablespoons extra virgin olive oil

2 garlic cloves

Zest of 2 lemons

Small bunch of mint or basil

1³/₄ ounces bottarga, freshly grated, plus extra to serve

14 ounces spaghetti

Sea salt and freshly ground black pepper

Bring a large saucepan of well-salted water to a boil.

Thinly slice the zucchini. Pour the oil into a large lidded skillet or saucepan and cook the zucchini on a medium-high heat until lightly browned and soft, about 15 minutes. Keeping the lid on makes them quicker to cook. Season with salt and pepper.

Menwhile, slice the garlic, zest the lemons, chop or tear the mint leaves, and grate the bottarga medium-fine.

When the zucchini is halfway through cooking, add the garlic to cook and soften and add the pasta to the boiling water, mixing well to prevent any strands from sticking together and cook until al dente.

When the zucchini is cooked, remove from the heat, add the lemon zest, mint, bottarga, salt and pepper. The bottarga slightly melts and becomes quite creamy. Add a dash of the pasta cooking water to loosen the sauce, mix well and set aside.

When the pasta is cooked, drain it, reserving a cupful of the water, and return the pasta to the pan off the heat.

Add the zucchini sauce to the pasta, mix well and add a little more of the reserved pasta water, if necessary, to loosen the sauce and prevent it from being too thick.

Check the seasoning, and serve immediately with extra bottarga grated over the top.

Tip: I serve up the pasta on plates, checking that each one has enough sauce before handing them round. The first plate always has less sauce than the last!

smoked eel and flageolet salad

SERVES 4
PREPARATION TIME 10 MINUTES MARINATING TIME 10 MINUTES

Smoked eel features in recipes in France and sometimes in Italy. This one is a simple, tasty salad. Other legumes—cannellini beans or chickpeas—can be substituted. I have used canned beans in this recipe for swiftness, but fresh or dried beans can be used instead.

14 ounces canned flageolet beans

1 garlic clove

5 ounces ripe tomatoes

1 small fennel, or ½ large one

2 tablespoons coarsely chopped mint leaves

2 tablespoons lemon juice

7 ounces smoked eel

4 tablespoons extra virgin olive oil

Bunch of watercress (about 4 large handfuls)

Sea salt and freshly ground black pepper

Rinse and drain the beans well. Set aside.

Smash the garlic with a little salt using a mortar and pestle or a knife. Add to a salad bowl. Cut the tomatoes into long thin slices. Halve the fennel bulb if using a whole one, remove and discard the tough triangular heart and thinly slice the rest. Coarsely chop the mint, juice the lemon, and cut the eel into chunky flakes.

Add the beans to the salad bowl then the tomatoes, fennel, mint, lemon, olive oil, eel, salt and pepper. Mix well.

Place the watercress on individual plates and scatter over the eel mixture. Serve immediately or, if you have time, leave to marinate for a few minutes to infuse the flavors.

egg and cheese dishes

Mediterranean cuisine has a wealth of recipes using eggs and different types of cheese, all of which are great for producing meals at speed. Eggs have been and remain a staple part of the diet because they are so versatile. From the simplest omelette or lightly baked egg sprinkled with cheese and herbs to more elaborate main courses or smart starters, eggs make it easy to produce delicious and often comforting meals in minutes.

There is a huge variety of cheeses, predominantly made with goat or sheep's milk as the terrain and the heat make many parts unsuitable for herds of dairy cows. A Mediterranean cheese board is an impressive sight at the end of a meal. Cheeses are fabricated to different stages of maturity: there are fresh soft cheeses such as French goat cheese which can be chalky or creamy; salty, crumbly feta, the sheep's cheese from Greece, Cyprus, and Turkey; ricottas from Italy and its islands. Mozzarella, made with cow's or buffalo's milk (the best), can be meltingly soft or there's an inferior firmer type which works best in cooking. But there are matured harder cheeses, such as the many manchegos of Spain or Italy's pecorino and, of course, Parmesan.

Cheeses are incorporated into salads and baked dishes, or the creamy varieties substituted for cream. Italians may use mascarpone or ricotta. The French have their slightly sour crème fraîche. In the southern Med yogurt is used extensively, especially in sauces for Turkish and Middle Eastern dishes. Blended with cornstarch (so that it doesn't separate), it is as versatile as cream, but a lot lighter.

eggs en cocotte

SERVES 4

PREPARATION TIME 15 MINUTES COOKING TIME 5–10 MINUTES

This is a traditional French recipe which, served with toast or warm crusty bread, makes a simple lunch dish or appetizer. Cooking times will vary depending on the thickness of the dish. I tend to use ramekins, but you can get cocotte molds.

2 tablespoons butter

1 medium leek, finely chopped, washed, and drained

4 large eggs

1 tablespoon tarragon

4 heaped tablespoons crème fraîche or heavy cream

Sea salt and freshly ground black pepper

Place 4 ramekins or cocotte molds in a high-sided roasting tray or gratin dish and preheat the oven to 300°F.

Melt the butter in a pan and cook the leeks gently for about 10 minutes until soft. Season with salt, pepper, and tarragon. Add the cream and bring to a gentle simmer.

Bring a kettle or pot of water to a boil.

Remove the ramekins from the oven and divide the leek mixture between them. Break an egg into each one, sprinkle a little salt and pepper on top, and place the ramekins in the tray on the middle rack of the oven. With the tray half out, carefully pour the boiling water around the ramekins, then slide back into the oven.

Cook for about 5–10 minutes until the center of the egg is still just soft. Remove carefully from the oven and take the ramekins out of the water.

Serve immediately.

fava beans with fresh cheese

SERVES 4–6

PREPARATION TIME: 25 MINUTES COOKING TIME: 5 MINUTES

Several of the tangy Mediterranean cheeses work well with fava beans: goat cheese in France, or a sheep's cheese—say pecorino in Italy or feta in Greece. Choose small young fresh fava beans. I like to peel the outer skins from just some of the beans to give a mixture of the beautiful pale gray and vibrant green inner bean as well. If you want to remove all the outer skins from the podded beans you need to allow more fava beans.

14 ounces fresh broad beans, podded weight (about 1³/₄ pounds unpodded weight)

Bunch of fresh herbs such as oregano, marjoram, mint, or thyme

2 tablespoons lemon juice

6 tablespoons good-quality extra virgin olive oil

4–5 ounces fresh goat cheese, pecorino, or feta cheese

Sea salt and freshly ground black pepper

Bring a large saucepan of salted water to a boil and blanch the fava beans for about 3 minutes. Drain and refresh under cold water. Leave to drain, then place on a dishcloth or paper towels to dry completely—this prevents the salad from being watery.

Peel the gray skin from at least the largest beans as the skin may be tough. Place in a bowl.

Make a dressing by crushing the herbs with a good pinch of salt in a mortar and pestle or food processor. Once the herbs are puréed, add the lemon juice, olive oil, and pepper. Add 1 heaped tablespoon of the dressing to the beans and mix well.

Transfer the beans to a plate, crumble cheese on top, and drizzle with the remaining herb sauce just before serving.

eggs cooked with yogurt, chili, and cilantro

SERVES 4
PREPARATION TIME 10 MINUTES COOKING TIME 5 MINUTES

This is a Turkish dish that makes a great snack or light lunch with a spicy twist. If you ever get to sample Turkish yogurt, it is wonderful. There are many different varieties: tam yali is the full-fat thick variety; suzme is strained, almost like a soft cheese. Adding cornstarch prevents the yogurt from separating.

1 large red chili

4 tablespoons chopped cilantro

1 large garlic clove

2 cups Greek-style yogurt

2 level teaspoons cornstarch

8 medium eggs

Sea salt

Preheat the broiler to high.

Chop the chili (remove the seeds if you prefer less heat) and cilantro. Smash the garlic with salt into a pulp and mix well with the yogurt and cornstarch.

Carefully crack the eggs without breaking the yolks into a gratin dish or ovenproof skillet to cover the bottom of the pan. Gently cover most of the eggs with dollops of the yogurt. Season with salt and scatter with the chili and cilantro.

Place under the broiler and cook for about 3–5 minutes until the whites are firm, but the yolks slightly runny.

Serve immediately with warm, thick Turkish-style bread.

frittata with bottarga and asparagus

SERVES 2 AS A MAIN COURSE, OR 6 AS AN APPETIZER WITH OTHER ANTIPASTI
PREPARATION TIME 5 MINUTES COOKING TIME 10 MINUTES

Frittata is a type of Italian omelet and bottarga is the roe of either mullet or tuna that is first cured then dried. The mullet roe has a more delicate flavor and is smaller in size. This is what I use for this recipe and for the Pasta with Zucchini (see page 75). It is popular in the southern fringes of Italy—especially Sicily—France, and Spain. You find bottarga in Italian delicatessans or, as an alternative, use chopped anchovies.

5 ounces asparagus, trimmed weight

6 eggs

2 tablespoons milk, optional

1 teaspoon coarsely chopped mint or flatleaf parsley

2 tablespoons extra virgin olive oil

2 heaped tablespoons coarsely grated bottarga

Sea salt and freshly ground pepper

Squeeze of lemon to serve

Bring a little water to a boil in a saucepan. Cut the asparagus stems in half lengthwise and, if long, cut them in half. Blanch for 2 minutes, then drain.

Preheat the broiler to high. Beat the eggs with the milk (if using), herbs, salt and pepper.

Heat a skillet to medium-hot. Add the olive oil and pour in the egg mixture. Scatter over the asparagus and cook for 2 minutes, until the bottom and sides are cooked.

Place the frittata under the broiler and briefly cook for about a minute, depending on the thickness, until the egg has just cooked.

Remove from the broiler and scatter with the grated bottarga. Serve immediately with a squeeze of lemon juice.

wilted spinach with serrano ham and eggs

SERVES 2 AS A MAIN COURSE OR 6 AS A TAPAS
PREPARATION TIME 10 MINUTES COOKING TIME 10 MINUTES

Eggs feature heavily in the cuisine of many Mediterranean countries. This recipe is similar to the famous Italian eggs florentine. I had this served in little ceramic tapas dishes with quail's eggs, which looks cute. But a medium-sized gratin dish or sauté pan works just as well. Serrano is a cured ham from Spain (the best is sold as jamon Iberico) similar to prosciutto which you can also use in this recipe.

1 pound large leaf spinach

2 tablespoons extra virgin olive oil

Pinch of nutmeg

2½–3½ ounces Serrano ham or prosciutto

4 medium eggs, or 6 quail's eggs

Sea salt and pepper

Wash the spinach discarding the larger stems if preferred. Bring a large saucepan with a little water to a boil. Add the spinach, mixing well until it just wilts, adding the spinach in stages if it won't all fit at once. Keep stirring until it is all just wilted. Drain well and, with the back of a large spoon, press down to release as much water as possible.

Preheat the broiler to high.

Rinse the pan, return to the heat to dry and add the olive oil. Add the drained spinach and season with nutmeg, salt and pepper. Mix well to infuse the flavors then transfer to a gratin dish or sauté pan and spread out.

Chop the ham into small pieces, sprinkle over the spinach. Break the eggs on top, season again, then lightly broil for 1–3 minutes, depending on size, until the eggs are just cooked, but still a little runny.

Serve with warm crusty bread.

baked mushrooms with prosciutto and goat cheese

SERVES 4
PREPARATION TIME 5 MINUTES COOKING TIME 15–20 MINUTES

Mushrooms shrink a lot when cooked, so do select large ones as two per person is about right unless you are serving other vegetables as well. However, if the mushrooms are really big they will take a little longer to cook. I find the tanginess of a mild, creamy goat cheese cuts the richness of the mushrooms and prosciutto. But mascarpone or ricotta are good substitutes.

6 tablespoons extra virgin olive oil

8 portabello mushrooms, stalks removed

2 garlic cloves

Small bunch of sage, leaves only (you need about 2 heaped tablespoons, chopped)

5 ounces mild, fresh creamy goat cheese

12 thin slices prosciutto

Sea salt and freshly ground pepper

Preheat the oven to 400°F.

Drizzle 1 tablespoon olive oil into a large gratin dish into which the mushrooms will fit snugly in a single layer. Wipe the mushrooms with paper towels. (Don't wash as mushrooms are porous and they will be too watery for this recipe.) Place them in the gratin dish, gills face-up.

Finely chop the garlic and sage (use a food processor for quickest results). Scatter over the mushrooms. Dollop the cheese on top of the mushrooms, about 3 heaped teaspoons per mushroom. Drizzle with the remaining oil, season with salt and pepper, and lay the prosciutto over the mushrooms. Cover with aluminum foil and cook in the oven for 10 minutes. Remove the foil and cook for another 5 minutes to crisp up the prosciutto.

Serve as a side dish with meat or on toast with salad as a starter.

briks with egg, fish, or meat

SERVES 6
PREPARATION TIME 20 MINUTES COOKING TIME 5–10 MINUTES

These little pastry parcels are sold on the streets of Morocco or served as a snack. Apart from egg, they may be filled with chopped fish or meat. Moroccans use a type of pastry called warkha leaves which I have finally noticed in some Middle Eastern stores. Phyllo dough is a good substitute, but you will need to use two sheets of it as it is thinner than warkha. Traditionally briks are formed into triangular shapes and deep fried, but I use a wok at home and even if they turn out flatter, they're just as tasty. Season generously as the pastry has no salt added to it. You might want to try this recipe out first before serving to guests, as you need to be able to gauge the heat of the oil accurately to ensure you don't overcook the pastry before the filling is cooked.

7 ounces fish fillet or ground lamb

1 clove garlic, chopped

½ teaspoon cumin seeds, ground

½ teaspoon coriander seeds, ground

½ teaspoon paprika

2 heaped tablespoons coarsely chopped cilantro

½ large red chili, finely chopped or

1 teaspoon chili flakes

6 warkha leaves or 12 small sheets of phyllo dough

cut about 8 inches wide

6 eggs

Sea salt

If using a food processor for the fish, blend it with the chopped garlic, and add the cumin and coriander seeds, paprika, and salt. Alternatively, smash the garlic with a little salt in a mortar and pestle or with the tip of a knife, finely chop the fish with a knife and mix by hand with the garlic and spices. If using ground lamb, mix with the smashed garlic and spices by hand. Set aside.

Chop the cilantro and chilli.

Heat the oil in a wok or use a deep fat fryer to medium high, 350°F or until a piece of bread dropped into the fat sizzles and browns in 30 seconds.

Place the pastry in a shallow bowl or soup plate (use two sheets if using phyllo) and break the egg in the middle. Scatter over a sixth of the fish or meat, a sprinkling of cilantro and chili, season with salt, and wrap up. You can do as the Moroccans do and fold over the pastry in half then half again into a triangular shape, or you can gather up the sides and bunch them together at the top if easier.

Carefully slip the briks into the hot oil and cook for about 3 minutes. I normally cook them for 2 minutes on one side, then turn them over for another minute.

Serve immediately but take care: they will be hot.

Tip: As warkha leaves are normally circular, you can trim your phyllo pastry into a circle first, but it's not necessary if time is limited.

pan-fried eggplant with feta, sesame seeds, and paprika

SERVES 4 AS A MEZZE
PREPARATION TIME 5–10 MINUTES COOKING TIME 20–25 MINUTES

This is a Greek-inspired dish. The acidity of the feta cuts the oiliness of the eggplant. If you have more time you might soak the eggplant in salted water for 15 minutes, then drain on paper towels to remove any bitterness. However, most varieties we buy are hothouse grown now, and it's not necessary, but eggplant will absorb less oil if pre-soaked. I have also used half sunflower oil and extra virgin olive oil, to make it lighter, but Mediterranean cooks would use all olive oil. It might seem a large amount, but eggplant soaks up a lot. It also depends on how large your skillet is, as the size determines the number of batches. Do ensure the eggplant is well cooked. They are not good undercooked.

About 1 cup olive oil and sunflower oil (50:50)

1 pound eggplant, trimmed and cut into ½ inch slices

3½ ounces feta cheese

1 tablespoon sesame seeds

Paprika

1 tablespoon coarsely chopped cilantro or mint leaves

Sea salt and freshly ground black pepper

Heat a large skillet or sauté pan with half the oil until medium high heat while you slice the eggplant. By using a generous amount of oil the eggplant fries, rather than burns, on the bottom of the pan. Add just enough slices to cover the bottom of the pan and cook on each side for about 4 minutes until golden brown and soft. Remove from the pan and drain on paper towels. Continue in batches until all the eggplant is cooked.

When the last batch of eggplant is in the pan, preheat the broiler to high.

Overlap the eggplant slices on a heatproof dish. Crumble over the feta. Sprinkle with the sesame seeds, salt, pepper, and paprika. Broil for 2 minutes until the feta is a light golden brown. Serve hot or cold with a scattering of herbs.

feta and chickpea salad with bell peppers and cilantro

SERVES 4 AS A STARTER, 2 AS A MAIN COURSE
PREPARATION TIME 20 MINUTES COOKING TIME 5 MINUTES

For speed, I've used ready broiled peppers in this recipe, but if you can't find any, you can substitute 4 medium tomatoes, cubed—although peppers taste better. You can also make this with cannellini or borlotti beans if you are not a fan of chickpeas.

7 ounces green beans

2 large red bell peppers, ready broiled, peeled, and seeded

2 heaped tablespoons cilantro leaves

14 ounces canned chickpeas, rinsed well and drained

1 large garlic clove

Scant ½ cup extra virgin olive oil

3 tablespoons lemon juice or red wine vinegar

4 large handfuls of arugula or other green salad

5 ounces feta cheese

12 black olives

Sea salt and freshly ground black pepper

Bring a saucepan of water to a boil while you trim and slice the green beans. Blanch the beans, then set aside to drain.

Cut the peppers into long thin strips and chop any large mint leaves. Rinse and drain the chickpeas well. Smash the garlic with salt.

Make a salad dressing with the garlic, olive oil, lemon juice, salt and pepper. Mix half the dressing with the chickpeas, add half the mint and leave to marinate until ready to serve.

Mix the arugula and green beans with the remaining salad dressing. Place the arugula and green beans on individual plates or a serving dish. Scatter over the chickpeas, then place the strips of pepper on top, then crumble with the feta cheese. Sprinkle over the olives and remaining mint. Serve immediately with warm Middle Eastern flatbread.

vegetables:
sides and mains

Anyone would happily be vegetarian in the Mediterranean, without having to worry about the balance of their diet, and still be equally inspired by the variety and interest of the dishes.

I marvel at how many Mediterranean recipes contain tomatoes or eggplant. The tomato comes, as they say, in all shapes and sizes. The different varieties seem to suit a particular dish or a method of cooking. Under-ripe green ones are used for salads; over-ripe, scented, thin-skinned plum tomatoes are prized for their juices. Then there's the giant "beefsteak" tomato, perfect for stuffing. Eggplant shows its versatility, too: baked, fried, broiled, or roasted. Puréed for appetizers, sliced or cubed for salads or stews. Combined with tomatoes they make one of the best culinary marriages, but they're just as happy to go with yogurt, lemon or spices.

In this section I concentrate on cooked recipes, leaving the raw to salads. These days more people are inclined to undercook vegetables to retain more crunch and vitamin content. The Mediterraneans are often perceived to take their time in life, a tradition they extend to cooking their vegetables. Although they don't boil them to death, rather, they use the minimum of water to keep the flavor (and nutrition) in the dish. So, where the list of ingredients and preparation time are kept to a minimum, I have been able to include many recipes that might be classified as slow cooked. For others I have chosen vegetables that take less time to cook. This chapter is definitely not just for vegetarians.

zucchini, pumpkin, and red bell pepper al forno

This is an attractive and easy mix of Mediterranean vegetables that can be put in the oven ("al forno" simply means cooked in the oven) and roasted while a piece of meat is roasting. But it would be equally good served with broiled or roasted fish.

1¼ pounds zucchini, washed

1¾ pounds pumpkin or butternut squash (1 pound peeled and seeded weight)

2 large red bell peppers

6 cloves garlic (cut in half if large)

3 sprigs rosemary

1 large red chili, seeded (optional)

6 tablespoons extra virgin olive oil

Sea salt and freshly ground black pepper

Preheat the oven to 400°F.

Cut the zucchini and pumpkin into largish cubes, cut at an angle. Trim and seed the peppers and cut them into large chunks. Place all the vegetables with the garlic in a large gratin dish or high-sided roasting pan. Chop the rosemary and chili (if using) and scatter over the vegetables. Season well with salt and pepper and drizzle over the extra virgin olive oil.

Toss the ingredients lightly together to coat in the oil and place in the oven for about 20 minutes, until the vegetables are cooked and light golden brown. Check the vegetables half way through cooking and turn over gently so that they are colored on all sides.

Serve with meat or fish.

broiled asparagus

This is a great simple dish for the spring months when we want to spend less time in the kitchen. Italians have a great many easy recipes that simply allow good-quality ingredients speak for themselves. This is a perfect example and an alternative to boiled asparagus. For best results use thin stalks served with oil and lemon for speed. If you only have large asparagus, I would suggest boiling the stalks for 2 minutes and serving with the saffron aioli. But broiled asparagus also works well with the aioli. It can be prepared in advance and the asparagus served either at room temperature or warm.

2 pounds good-quality asparagus (or 1¼ pounds if very thin asparagus is available)

Sea salt and freshly ground black pepper

to serve

Drizzle of olive oil

Juice of lemon, or saffron aioli (see page 45)

If using thick asparagus, blanch the stalks in boiling water for 1 minute, refresh in cold water and drain on paper towels; then griddle briefly on both sides until lightly browned. If very thin asparagus is available no pre-cooking is needed. Preheat the griddle and grill the raw asparagus stalks until light brown. Place in a bowl, season with salt and pepper, and cover with plastic wrap to steam gently.

Drizzle with the olive oil and serve with some lemon juice or aioli.

Tip: If you don't have a griddle, preheat the broiler and cook the asparagus on all sides until soft and light brown.

deep-fried artichokes

SERVES 4
PREPARATION TIME 10 MINUTES COOKING TIME 10 MINUTES

This is an easy side dish or appetizer to prepare when young artichokes are available as you don't have to remove the hairy choke from the center. Sometimes they are cooked whole, but you might find it easier to cut them up as I suggest.

2 cups sunflower oil

6 small young artichokes (about 1¼ pounds)

Sea salt and freshly ground black pepper

1 lemon, cut into slices

Heat the oil in a wok or deep fat fryer to medium-high (350°F or until a cube of bread dropped into the fat sizzles and browns in 30 seconds).

Cut the stem of the artichoke, leaving about 1 inch intact if young and tender. Remove the first and second row of leaves around the base of the artichokes. Trim about a third off the top of the artichokes. Cut the artichokes in quarters or sixths, depending on size. (Only prepare them when you are ready to add them to the pan otherwise they tend to discolor.)

Add about half the artichokes to the pan. Cook for about 3–5 minutes, depending on size, until the heart is soft and the outer leaves crispy. Prepare the rest while the first batch is cooking. Then add and cook in the same way.

Drain the artichokes on paper towels, sprinkle with salt and pepper and squeeze lemon juice over them just before serving.

green beans braised with tomatoes and basil

SERVES 2
PREPARATION TIME 5 MINUTES COOKING TIME 10 MINUTES

In the Mediterranean most vegetables are generally either served raw or slow cooked. This is a great way to serve green beans when tomatoes are at their best. Use cherry tomatoes if ordinary ones aren't ripe enough. Delicious served with fish or meat.

9 ounces tomatoes

3 tablespoons extra virgin olive oil

1 large garlic clove

7 ounces green beans

2 tablespoons basil leaves, coarsely chopped or torn

Sea salt and freshly ground black pepper

Cut the tomatoes into chunks, each about ½ inch in size.

Pour the oil into a lidded sauté pan and heat to medium-high. Slice the garlic and cook until golden brown. Add the tomatoes, salt and pepper, and cook briefly while you trim the beans.

Place the prepared beans on top of the tomatoes, cover the pan and cook gently for 5 minutes. Remove the lid and stir well to check the bottom of the pan isn't burning. Add the torn or chopped basil and stir, ensuring the green beans are immersed in the tomato sauce. Cover with the lid again and gently cook for a further 5 minutes, until the green beans are tender and the sauce well reduced. Add a dash of water if the beans are not cooked through.

Let rest for a few minutes to infuse the flavor.

VEGETABLES

95

carrots with cumin

SERVES 4
PREPARATION TIME 5 MINUTES COOKING TIME 15–20 MINUTES

The more water you use the quicker the carrots cook, but the flavor is far less intense than if you just use the condensation from the saucepan lid. A little parsley sprinkled on top brings out the color of this dish.

2 pounds carrots

4 tablespoons extra virgin olive oil

2 garlic cloves

1 level or heaped teaspoon cumin seeds,

depending on freshness

Sea salt and freshly ground black pepper

Peel the carrots and thinly slice, by hand, or in a machine for the quickest results.

Pour the olive oil into a large lidded skillet and add the carrots, cooking on a medium-high heat. Chop the garlic and, for best flavor, coarsely grind the cumin seed, but this is not essential if you don't have a mortar and pestle or spice grinder. Add the garlic and cumin to the pan, and mix briefly to lightly brown the garlic. Season with salt and pepper, reduce the heat to low and cover with a lid. Cook for another 15 minutes, stirring occasionally so the garlic doesn't burn and the carrots cook evenly. When lifting the lid, make sure any water from condensation drops into the saucepan to moisten the carrots. Add a few tablespoons of water toward the end if the carrots are not cooked.

You can prepare these carrots in advance and reheat before serving. Delicious with simply roasted or broiled lamb or fish.

pumpkin with chili and nutmeg

SERVES 4
PREPARATION TIME 10 MINUTES COOKING TIME 20 MINUTES

Pumpkin is part of the squash family. The Italians call it zucca—a large cousin to the zucchini. Apart from its sweet taste, it adds great color. But experiment with all the different varieties, as some are tasteless and watery. Butternut or acorn are two reliable ones. Cooking in oil instead of boiling intensifies its flavor. Chili works really well with pumpkin, cutting its sweetness, and the red varieties are picked out beautifully against the orange of the pumpkin.

Pumpkin is a good substitute for potatoes (less starchy) and it works well with roast meats. The texture of the final dish depends on the variety used. Some go into a mash, others are firmer and keep their shape more.

2 pounds pumpkin (butternut squash is good)

2 tablespoons extra virgin olive oil

1 large garlic clove, sliced

½ large red chili (optional)

Good pinch of nutmeg, freshly grated if possible

Sea salt and freshly ground black pepper

Peel the pumpkin and remove the seeds, scooping them out with a spoon is the easiest way. Chop the pumpkin into small cubes.

Heat a large lidded saucepan and add the oil. Slice the garlic and chili (if using), removing the seeds if you prefer less heat. Add them to the pan along with the pumpkin, nutmeg, salt and pepper.

Stir the pumpkin to glaze it in oil and spices and cover the pan. Cook on a low heat, stirring occasionally to prevent the base of the pan from burning, for 15–20 minutes. Allow the condensation from the lid to drip into the pan as you lift it, because this helps to speed up the cooking. When the pumpkin is soft, serve hot.

This can be prepared in advance and reheated just before serving.

sautéed spring vegetables with yogurt and mint

SERVES 4
PREPARATION TIME 10 MINUTES COOKING TIME 10 MINUTES

This is a great dish to serve with a simple piece of broiled fish or chicken. It is really good to make in the spring months using fresh peas, but they will take longer to prepare and cook.

½ cup low-fat yogurt

1 heaped teaspoon cornstarch

2 tablespoons extra virgin olive oil

3½ ounces scallions, finely chopped

7 ounces frozen peas

¼ cup water

8 ounces washed and trimmed baby spinach

3 tablespoons fresh mint, coarsely chopped

Sea salt and freshly ground black pepper

Prepare all the ingredients so they are ready to cook quickly. Mix the yogurt with the cornstarch. Add the oil to a nonstick, preferably high-sided, skillet and cook the scallions for a few minutes until soft. Add the peas and coat in the olive oil, then add the water and cook the peas for a few minutes. (Fresh peas take longer than frozen and you might need to add a little more water if they are still not cooked and the water has evaporated.)

Add the washed baby leaf spinach and cook briefly until wilted, stirring frequently. Season with salt and pepper and add the mint and yogurt mixed with cornstarch. Stir briefly and remove from the heat. Serve immediately.

roasted eggplant with sumac

SERVES 2
PREPARATION TIME 10 MINUTES COOKING TIME 20–30 MINUTES

Many eggplant dishes are slow cooked, but here is one of the few recipes that got in under the 30-minute rule. I roasted the eggplant, but it can be fried as well. Sumac accents Turkish, Syrian, and Lebanese cuisine. This spice adds a tart lemony flavor, so you can substitute lemon juice if you can't find sumac.

1 large eggplant (about 1 pound)

8 tablespoons extra virgin olive oil

1 tablespoon sumac

1 heaped tablespoon chopped scallions

1 heaped tablespoon chopped cilantro or parsley

Sea salt and freshly ground black pepper

Preheat the oven to 400°F.

Trim, then slice the eggplant into disks about a finger-width thick. Drizzle 3 tablespoons of the oil over the bottom of a roasting pan and spread out the eggplant slices on top. Drizzle 3 more tablespoons of oil over the eggplant. Season with sumac, salt and pepper and bake in the oven for about 20–30 minutes, until soft.

Meanwhile, put the chopped scallions and herbs in a serving bowl. When the eggplant is cooked, add to the bowl with the remaining olive oil if needed, check the seasoning and serve.

Tip: This can also be left to marinate and served at room temperature.

VEGETABLES

99

braised zucchini with olives

SERVES 4
PREPARATION TIME 10 MINUTES COOKING TIME 20 MINUTES

This is a nice dish to serve with simply broiled fish. I have also turned it into a pasta sauce. To speed up the preparation I use pitted olives. But not the grim cheap ones soaked in brine. Try to track down good-quality ones to make the flavor work. Alternatively smashing them between your fingers or with the flat of a knife will remove the pit very quickly and easily. I suggest adding some good-quality red wine vinegar to cut the oil.

4 tablespoons extra virgin olive oil

1 large red onion

1½ pounds zucchini

1 large garlic clove

3½ ounces black olives

3 tablespoons coarsely chopped mint leaves

2 tablespoons red wine vinegar (optional)

Sea salt and freshly ground black pepper

Pour the oil into a large sauté pan or skillet and coarsely chop the onion. Cook the onion on a medium heat, stirring occasionally.

Wash and trim the zucchini and chop the garlic. Halve the zucchini lengthwise, then slice and add to the pan with the garlic. Season with salt and pepper and cook for about 15 minutes until soft and lightly caramelized.

Meanwhile, pitt and coarsely chop the olives and chop the mint. Add the olives, mint, and vinegar (if using) at the last minute and mix.

This can be served either hot or at room temperature.

braised cabbage with bacon and nutmeg

SERVES 4
PREPARATION TIME 15 MINUTES COOKING TIME 15 MINUTES

If you have been put off cabbage, try this recipe. The trick to successful green cabbage is to cook it briefly. Flavoring it with bacon and nutmeg complements it perfectly. I have used Savoy, but any greens will work just as well and may take less time. Add a dash of cream for some decadence—this works surprisingly well with white firm fish such as turbot or monkfish. Also try to slice the cabbage really thinly so it reminds you more of a restaurant than the school cafeteria!

1¼ pounds Savoy cabbage

2 tablespoons extra virgin olive oil

5 ounces bacon or pancetta, sliced or diced

1 large garlic clove

1 heaped tablespoon chopped sage or rosemary leaves

Good pinch of nutmeg

Sea salt and freshly ground black pepper

Remove the outer leaves of the cabbage and wash them if dirty or trim if wilting. Cut in half, removing any thick stems. Then finely slice. Quarter the remaining cabbage, remove the thick core, and finely slice.

Add the oil and bacon to a large lidded saucepan and cook on a high heat until light golden brown. Chop the garlic and sage, turn the heat to low, and add them to the pan. Cook briefly, then add the cabbage, adding a splash of water if you think the cabbage might brown. Season with nutmeg, salt and pepper. Cover the pan and cook gently for another 10 minutes, stirring occasionally, and adding a dash more water if it's sticking on the bottom. You want the cabbage to retain its nice bright green color.

Serve immediately—you can reheat it, but the color may fade!

saffron potatoes with red onions

SERVES 4

PREPARATION TIME 10 MINUTES COOKING TIME 20 MINUTES

A side dish to serve with meat or fish. The saffron makes the potatoes a lovely yellow color, and if you can, buy red onions because the colors work well together. Use waxy, boiling potatoes rather than floury, baking ones, since they don't break up when cooked.

2 pounds waxy potatoes

Good pinch of saffron

10 ounces red onions

1 garlic clove

3 tablespoons extra virgin olive oil

Sea salt and freshly ground black pepper

1 tablespoon coarsely chopped flatleaf parsley (optional)

Bring a large saucepan of salted water to a boil.

Peel the potatoes and cut into longish wedges, depending on their size. Cook the potatoes with the saffron and cook for about 15 minutes, until soft. Drain and set aside.

Meanwhile, cut the onions in half then slice them. Slice the garlic. Pour the oil into a sauté or skillet and heat to medium-hot. Cook the onion with the garlic for about 10–15 minutes until soft.

Add the potatoes, season with salt and pepper, and cook for another 5–10 minutes to amalgamate the flavors and lightly seal the potatoes in the oil.

Serve hot or cold, garnished with a sprinkling of parsley if you wish.

patatas bravas

SERVES 4

PREPARATION TIME 10 MINUTES COOKING TIME 20 MINUTES

This classic Spanish recipe is well worth attempting and is often served as tapas, but works equally well as a vegetable side dish. If you wish to omit the chorizo then do, but the smoky flavor permeates the potatoes really well. If you are using a hot chorizo you might want to omit the chili. Use waxy potatoes to prevent them from breaking up when cooking.

1 medium onion, quartered and sliced

2½ ounces chorizo

3 tablespoons extra-virgin olive oil

1 pound large waxy potatoes

1 large garlic clove, coarsely chopped

1 level teaspoon dried chili, finely chopped

4 tablespoons canned chopped tomatoes

1 heaped teaspoon paprika

Sea salt

Cut up the onion and chorizo. Add to a sauté pan with the olive oil and cook on a medium heat for 5 minutes. Peel the potatoes while the onion is cooking and cut into ½ inch cubes. Add to the onion mixture and stir well to coat the potatoes in the oil and prevent them from sticking to the bottom of the pan. Add the garlic and chili, season with salt, and cook for 5 minutes.

Add the tomatoes and paprika, mix well, cover with a lid, and cook for 15 minutes longer. Stir frequently to prevent the bottom of the pan from sticking.

Check to see that the potatoes are soft. You can serve them immediately but they do taste even better if left for 15 minutes for the flavors to infuse.

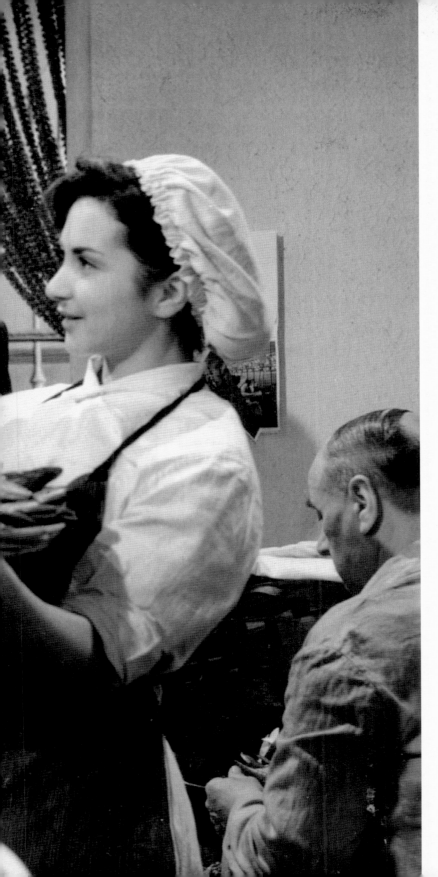

fish and seafood

No one could write a book on Mediterranean cuisine without including fish and seafood and for this chapter it was a hard task to select what to include from the wealth of potential recipes. Fish, unlike many cuts of meat, cooks fast. From tiny anchovies and sardines to huge tuna steaks and whole sea bass, and clams, octopus, shrimp, squid, and lobster too—the Mediterranean offers cooks real scope.

There are a few omissions imposed by the 30-minute rule. Complex fish soups such as French bouillabaisse cannot be included. Also, I wanted to show more unusual recipes as well as some of the easy ones that most books ignore. Lobster, for example, is obviously a classic and stylish treat, but many books don't give instruction on how to cook it as so often lobster is sold ready cooked. Sadly, too many fishmongers overcook it. I show you how to do it properly.

An essential point to keep in mind when buying fish is its freshness. Choosing the freshest is far more important that the actual type of fish: you can often substitute one for another, provided you substitute like for like, so, if a recipe calls for oily fish such as a sardine, you could use mackerel. Equally a recipe requiring flat fish could be made with sole or turbot; a round fish could be bream or sea bass; tuna and swordfish steaks are also interchangeable.

Fish is cooked very simply: broiled, deep-fried, poached, or baked. A little olive oil, a wedge of lemon, a few herbs, and you have the Mediterranean on your plate. Take a look at the sauces section: a dollop of any of those recipes will go perfectly with a piece of broiled or baked fish, too.

baked red mullet with grape leaves

SERVES 2 AS A MAIN COURSE
PREPARATION TIME 5 MINUTES COOKING TIME 10 MINUTES

This could be described as a quintessential Mediterranean dish. Fish, grape leaves, and lemons: bastions of the region, all three in abundance. If you happen to have access to fresh grape leaves that's perfect. But I made this dish with the easier to source grape leaves in brine. They are sold in jars, usually to make dolmades, and are available in supermarkets. This dish is perfect cooked over charcoal, if you have time.

2–4 red mullet or 2 x 1¼-pound sea bream

Several sprigs of thyme or rosemary

1 lemon

4–6 grape leaves, depending on size, fresh or canned

Drizzle of extra virgin olive oil for cooking and serving

Ask your fishmonger to scale and gut the fish for you but leave on the heads and tails. Wash them thoroughly, inside and out. If using grape leaves in brine, rinse well. Drain on paper towels.

Cover a baking sheet with aluminum foil, place in the oven and preheat to 400°F.

Stuff the cavity of the fish with a sprig of thyme and a slice of lemon. Drizzle no more than 1 teaspoon of olive oil over each fish.

Place the grape leaves, with the veins facing down, on a counter. Place the fish on top (you may need to use 2 or 3 overlapping leaves, depending on their size). It looks attractive if you keep the head and tail showing. Wrap up the fish, glaze with some olive oil, and place sealed-side down on the preheated baking sheet. Top with slices of lemon. Bake for about 10 minutes, depending on the size of the fish.

Transfer to a plate, drizzle with extra virgin olive oil and serve immediately.

mussels with curry

SERVES 4 AS AN APPETIZER, OR 2 AS A MAIN COURSE
PREPARATION TIME 10 MINUTES COOKING TIME 20 MINUTES

Mussels are served all along the coasts of France and there are many variations of the classic moules marinière. If you wish to keep it simple, just omit the curry paste. But the French love to pop a little curry paste (as opposed to powder) into a lot of their fish sauces. The color of the yellow sauce and the orange mussels with a splash of green from the parsley looks beautiful. Don't be tempted to add more curry paste though—the flavor should be subtle.

2 pounds really fresh mussels

1 small white onion

1 large garlic clove

3 tablespoons extra virgin olive oil

1 teaspoon mild curry paste

¾ cup white wine

2 tablespoons heavy cream

2 heaped tablespoons coarsely chopped flatleaf parsley

Soak the mussels in plenty of cold water.

Gently heat a lidded sauté pan or saucepan large enough to accommodate all the mussels on the bottom of the pan (or you can cook them in batches). Finely chop the onion and garlic. Add the olive oil, onion, and garlic to the pan, cover, and cook gently for about 10 minutes until soft.

Meanwhile tug off the beard, or hairy attachment to the mussels, pulling with your hand. (No need to worry too much about any white barnacles; provided there is no dirt on the shells, they won't need to be scrubbed.) As you clean the mussels, drain in a colander over a bowl.

When the onion is soft, and the mussels are ready for cooking, add the curry paste to the pan, mix and cook for 1 minute, then turn up the heat to high. As soon as the onion starts to bubble, but before it burns, add the mussels. Let them come up to a high heat again for 1 minute, then add the wine, cover the pan, and cook for 5 minutes. Stir the mussels once, to ensure they cook evenly and the ones on top have a chance to cook and open up.

Once the mussels are opened, remove. If you find most have opened, remove those first, allowing the remaining ones a chance to open up. Pour the mussels and the onion mixture back into a colander over a bowl to catch the liquid. (If you are cooking in batches, use half the wine and cook the remaining mussels in the rest of the wine. They don't need the onion mixture; that is mixed later.)

When all the mussels are cooked, divide between large warm bowls. Tip the reserved juices back into the pan, being careful to discard the gritty sediment at the bottom of the bowl. Add the heavy cream, bring to a boil, and add the parsley. Pour the juice over the mussels and eat immediately with warm crusty bread to soak up the juices.

baked sea bream with fennel and chili

SERVES 2
PREPARATION TIME 15 MINUTES COOKING TIME 10 MINUTES

"En papillotte" is a French term for baking fish in a parcel. Traditionally parchment paper would be used, but foil is much easier to seal. The trick is to be generous with the space around the fish; as it cooks steam is formed in the bag and puffs it up. Don't overpack the pan if you wish to do this recipe for larger numbers. Make sure the fish pieces are the same size so they cook within the same time. The thicker and denser the fish the longer it will take. The parcels can be prepared in advance, but the spinach must be cooled completely before adding to the fish.

2 x 6-ounce fillets round fish such as sea bream or mullet, boned and filleted

2 tablespoons extra virgin olive oil

8 ounces baby spinach, ready washed

1 small fennel bulb (3½ ounces)

1 tablespoon coarsely chopped dill

½ large red chili, seeded and chopped

2 tablespoons white wine or lemon juice

Sea salt and freshly ground black pepper

Put a large baking sheet in the oven and preheat to 400°F.

Add 1 tablespoon olive oil to a large saucepan and add the spinach. Season with salt and pepper and cook over medium heat until just wilted. Place in a sieve over a bowl to drain and set aside.

To slice the fennel very finely I use the large holes of a grater. Grate it into a bowl and add the chopped dill, season with salt and pepper, add half the chopped chili, mix well and check for seasoning.

Place 2 pieces of foil (the heavy duty type is best) large enough to enclose the fish on a clean counter. Place ½ tablespoon oil about three-quarters of the way up each piece (this will become the middle of one side when folded over!) Put half the spinach on the oil on each piece. Divide the fennel mixture and place on top. Finally place a fillet of fish on top, season with salt and pepper and the remaining chopped chili. Drizzle each fish with 1 tablespoon wine or lemon juice then the remaining ½ tablespoon olive oil.

Fold the foil over and seal the edges very well, starting with the sides and ending with the top, so that no juices or air can escape during cooking.

Place the packages on the hot baking sheet and cook for about 10–15 minutes. If the foil is well sealed your package will puff up once it is cooked. You can always check one package first to see the fish is cooked and reseal if it needs a few minutes longer.

Serve with boiled potatoes or warm crusty bread.

broiled seafood with chilies

SERVES 6
PREPARATION TIME 15 MINUTES COOKING TIME 5–10 MINUTES

Broiled squid with chili is probably one of the signature dishes of the River Café and I remember preparing tons of it when I worked there. The freshness of the squid works perfectly with the chili. Broiled fish is an easy and quintessential Mediterranean recipe. Using a mixture of fish is a great idea for antipasti. Here I have used just shrimp and squid but you could have little mullet, sardines, or anchovies. Ask the fishmonger to clean and cut the squid, explaining that it is for broiling flat. But you have the instructions here if this is not possible.

6 medium squid, cleaned

6 large raw shrimp, shelled, heads on or off

2 large red chilies

1 heaped tablespoon coarsely chopped flatleaf parsley

6–8 tablespoons estate bottled extra virgin olive oil

Sea salt and freshly ground black pepper

Extra virgin olive oil for broiling

to serve

Arugula leaves

6 wedges of lemon

To clean the squid, pull the heads and tentacles from the bodies with any innards. Remove the transparent vertebrae and cut down the ridge that remains, so that the squid is completely flat on a cutting board. Scrape away any sand and innards from the middle. Cut the heads off below the eyes and discard, leaving just the tentacles. Rinse the squid thoroughly in cold water, making sure any sand is removed, particularly from in the suckers. Leave to drain in a colander for a few minutes.

Using a serrated knife lightly score the inner side of the squid, in a criss-cross pattern. Be careful not to cut through the flesh.

Wash the shrimp well and dry on paper towels.

Preheat a griddle or broiler to hot.

Make the sauce by seeding (if you prefer less heat) and finely chopping the chilies. Place in a bowl with the parsley, olive oil, and salt. Lightly oil the squid and shrimp with oil and season with salt and pepper.

Add the shrimp to the griddle or broiler and cook for 3–5 minutes, depending on their size. Set aside.

Place the squid, scored-side down on the griddle, and cook briefly for about 1 minute or less on each side. As the squid is turned over it will start to curl up, but by then it is ready to be removed.

Serve the squid immediately with the shrimp, arugula, chili sauce, and a wedge of lemon squeezed over.

sardines with chermoula sauce

SERVES 6
PREPARATION TIME 15 MINUTES COOKING TIME 5–15 MINUTES

Chermoula (or Charmoulah) is a classic Moroccan marinade or sauce used with fish as well as poultry. If you have time, roast the cumin and coriander in a dry skillet before grinding. The flavor is much more intense.

24 sardines, boned and flattened out, or about 2½ pounds other oily fish such as red mullet or sea bream, cleaned and gutted

for the stuffing

3 heaped tablespoons coarsely chopped flatleaf parsley

3 heaped tablespoons coarsely chopped cilantro

2 garlic cloves

1 heaped tablespoon freshly ground cumin seeds

1 heaped tablespoon freshly ground coriander seeds

1 tablespoons sweet paprika

½ large red chili, finely chopped

⅓ cup extra virgin olive oil plus extra for greasing

Juice of 1 lemon (3 tablespoons)

Sea salt and freshly ground black pepper

Place a large baking tray in the oven and preheat to 400°F.

Smash the garlic with a little salt and finely chop the herbs and spices together (or you can put all the ingredients in a food processor). Stir in the oil, lemon juice, pepper, and extra salt if need be.

Prepare the sardines if possible keeping the tail attached, flattening the fish so that both sides lie side by side. If the fish is damp, drain first on paper towels. Place half the flattened sardines onto a piece of greased foil. Lightly season the fish with salt and spread a spoonful of chermoula sauce over each one. Place a similar sized sardine on top of the first sardine and season the top sardine with salt. Continue until all the sardines are prepared.

If using a whole large fish, score the skin of the fish several times, cutting slits on both sides of the fish, down through the flesh to the bone. Spoon chermoula over and inside the fish, reserving a few tablespoons to serve once cooked.

Bake the fish in the oven for 5–10 minutes for the sardines and up to 15 minutes for larger fish, depending on the size. You can tell when a large fish is cooked when the eye goes opaque, or the color of poached eggs.

Serve immediately with some lightly dressed arugula and warm flatbread.

sea bass stuffed with prunes and tamarind

SERVES 4
PREPARATION TIME 15 MINUTES COOKING TIME 15 MINUTES

This is a Syrian dish that works for any round fish that is very fresh. The tartness of the tamarind combines well with the sweetness of the prunes. Substitute other dried fruits if you prefer. The recipe normally has the fish stuffed with rice as well, but this would take too long to prepare for our purposes. I also selected two smallish fish so they take less time to cook. But a larger one works just as well, just increase the cooking time. Serve with plain or saffron rice.

2 x 1-pound sea bass, sea bream or other round fish

1 ounce almonds

6 tablespoons extra virgin olive oil

1 ounce pinenuts

1 small red onion, finely chopped

1 garlic clove chopped

1 heaped teaspoon freshly grated ginger

Small pinch of saffron

2½ ounces pitted prunes

Zest and juice of 1 large lime (about 4 tablespoons of juice)

2 heaped teaspoons tamarind paste

3 tablespoon brown sugar

2 tablespoons coarsely chopped cilantro

Sea salt and freshly ground black pepper

Ask the fishmonger to scale, gut, and clean the fish. Rinse the fish inside and out just before cooking to remove any remaining blood. Set aside on paper towels to drain.

Put a baking sheet in the oven and preheat to 400°F.

Gently heat a lidded sauté pan or skillet. Coarsely chop the almonds and add 2 tablespoons of the oil to the pan, along with the almonds and pinenuts. Finely chop the onion and garlic and grate the ginger, adding each ingredient to the pan as you go. Cover the pan and cook over a medium-high heat until the nuts are light golden brown and the onions are soft.

Meanwhile soak the saffron in 1 tablespoon water and chop the prunes into quarters. When the onions are soft, add the saffron liquid, prunes, lime juice, tamarind, and sugar. Mix briefly over the heat then remove and set aside.

Cut 2 pieces of aluminum foil large enough to enclose each fish. Place them on the counter and drizzle 1 tablespoon of the oil in the center of each sheet to prevent the fish from sticking too much. Place the fish on top. Divide the onion mixture between the two fish, placing some inside the cavity and the rest on top. Drizzle the remaining tablespoon of oil over the fish. Season with salt and pepper and scatter ½ tablespoon cilantro over each fish and 1 tablespoon water over each. Wrap up the fish and seal the foil tightly so no air can escape.

Place the fish on the preheated baking sheet and cook for about 15 minutes. Carefully open one foil parcel to check if the fish is just cooked—the eye should look opaque, or the color of poached eggs. Return to the oven for a few minutes longer if it is not ready.

Serve with the remaining cilantro sprinkled over both fish.

fish patties

SERVES 4 AS A MAIN COURSE, OR 6 AS A GENEROUS APPETIZER
(MAKES 16–20 BALLS)
PREPARATION TIME 20 MINUTES COOKING TIME 10 MINUTES

These deep-fried morsels are found in Morocco and Eygpt. They are
eaten dunked in harissa (recipe on page 42) or just squeezed with lemon
juice. Do dry-roast the spices if you can—it brings out their flavor, making
them nuttier. If you have any of the mixture left over, you can use it to
make the briks on page 87.

1 pound white fish such as sea bream

1 heaped teaspoon cumin seeds

1 heaped teaspoon coriander seeds

½ large chili

1 large garlic clove

2 tablespoons fresh breadcrumbs

2 heaped tablespoons coarsely chopped cilantro

1 cup sunflower oil

Sea salt and freshly ground black pepper

Lemon wedges for serving

Bone and skin the fish, or get your fishmonger to do it for you. Rinse the
fish in cold water and pat dry with paper towels.

If you have time, lightly toast the cumin seeds and coriander seeds in a
dry skillet. Grind the cumin and coriander in a mortar and pestle or spice
grinder. Chop the chili and garlic.

Place the fish in a food processor with the cumin, coriander, chili,
garlic, breadcrumbs, and cilantro. Season well with salt and pepper
and mix well.

Heat a skillet with the sunflower oil to medium–high.

Roll the mixture into 16–20 balls, each weighing about 1 ounce, then
flatten them a little. Set aside.

When you have rolled half the mixture, start to cook the patties without
crowding the pan, cooking for about 2 minutes on each side. As they
cook, roll the rest of the mixture and cook as a second batch.

Place the fish patties onto paper towels to drain.

Serve warm with a squeeze of lemon juice and harissa sauce if you wish.

Tip: To check you have seasoned correctly, try cooking 1 small patty first,
then taste, adding more salt if necessary.

broiled swordfish
with tapenade

SERVES 4
PREPARATION TIME 15 MINUTES COOKING TIME 2–5 MINUTES

A very simple but delicious dish. Swordfish is found in abundance in the coastal towns of Sicily. Catania on the east coast has the most amazing fish market where swordfish and tuna are sold regularly. And Palermo, the capital, is equally amazing for fresh fish. Tapenade is an olive paste common to both Italy and the south of France. It can be also served with pasta or spread on crostini as an antipasti.

4 x 5-ounce swordfish or tuna steaks or other firm-fleshed fish

Drizzle of sunflower oil for cooking

Sea salt and freshly ground black pepper

for the tapenade

8 ounces good-quality black olives, pitted

½ cup extra virgin olive oil

1 small garlic clove, coarsely chopped

1 tablespoon flatleaf parsley or basil

4 anchovy fillets

2 tablespoons lemon juice

1 teaspoon of capers

Sea salt and freshly ground black pepper

Place all the ingredients for the tapenade into a food processor and whizz into a purée.

Preheat a griddle or broiler.

Pat dry the swordfish steaks with paper towels and lightly brush them with the oil. Season with salt and pepper and sear on a high heat until the fish is just cooked, about 2 minutes either side, depending on the thickness of the steaks. If you prefer them completely cooked through, cook a little longer.

Place the swordfish on a plate, draining on paper towels if very oily and drizzle over the sauce.

Serve with boiled broccolini to mop up the tapenade.

Tip: It's quite hard to tell if the fish is ready apart from just bending the center of one steak to check it is correctly cooked. Turn it over when serving—no one will notice.

skate with caper and parsley sauce

SERVES 2
PREPARATION TIME 10 MINUTES COOKING TIME 5 MINUTES

This is a classic dish that is simple yet sophisticated. Skate is the traditional choice but another firm white fish such as cod, halibut, or sea bass can equally be used. Serve with boiled potatoes or lentils.

2 pieces of skate wing (each weighing about 7 ounces)

1 heaped tablespoon capers, drained

2 level tablespoons coarsely chopped flatleaf parsley

4 tablepoons extra virgin olive oil

Juice of 1 lemon

Sea salt and freshly ground black pepper

Lemon wedges for serving

Trim the skate if necessary by removing the front thick bone and cut away the tips of the wings.

Rinse the capers, squeeze dry and coarsely chop. Coarsely chop the parsley then mix with the capers and set aside.

Heat a large skillet and add 2 tablespoons of the oil. Cook the skate over a medium-high heat, cooking for about 3 minutes on each side. Lower the heat if you find the skate is cooking too quickly before cooking through.

When the fish is cooked, place on warm plates. Add the remaining olive oil to the pan, add the capers, parsley, and lemon juice and heat until bubbling. Remove from the heat, season with salt and pepper, pour over the skate, and serve immediately with lemon wedges.

deep-fried fish

SERVES 4 AS AN APPETIZER, OR 2 AS A MAIN COURSE
PREPARATION TIME 10 MINUTES COOKING TIME 5–10 MINUTES

Deep-fried fish—"fritto misto", "frîture de poisson", "pescado frito", or "psarotigania"—is often on menus in coastal towns throughout the Med. Mostly little fish or rings of calamari (squid) are best-suited to this method of cooking. A mixture of different fish spread out on a large platter with lots of lemon wedges and a chilled glass of crisp white wine is a great way to start a meal, or have as a main course. The key to success lies in the batter or flour. After discussing it with a few chefs, the best flour to use is a coarse one, such as fine semolina, or the Spanish have a wheat flour called Harina de Trigo. It's vital to get the oil temperature right, too, so that the fish is cooked through by the time it is browned on the outside.

1¼ pounds mixed fish such as baby mullet, sardines, anchovies, baby sole, guernard, squid

2 cups sunflower oil or 50:50 olive oil and sunflower oil

⅓ cup milk

1¼ cups fine semolina or Harina de Trigo

Lemon wedges to serve

Ask the fishmonger to scale, gut, and clean the fish. Rinse the fish inside and out just before cooking to remove any remaining blood. Set aside on paper towels to drain.

Heat the oil in a deep-fat fryer or wok to medium-hot, 350°F, or until a piece of bread dropped into the fat sizzles and browns in 30 seconds.

Place the milk in a medium gratin dish or large plate. Place the semolina in a similar-sized dish or plate. Coat the fish first in the milk then lightly dust with semolina.

When the oil is hot enough, add the fish, in batches, so the temperature of the oil doesn't drop too much. Deep-fry each batch for about 2–4 minutes, depending on their size. Remove with a slotted spoon and drain on paper towels. Continue until all the fish is used up.

Serve hot with wedges of lemon—on thick parchment paper is the most authentic way.

pan-fried scallops with bacon and sherry vinegar

SERVES 2 AS A MAIN COURSE, 4 AS AN APPETIZER
PREPARATION TIME 10 MINUTES COOKING TIME 10 MINUTES

Scallops with bacon is a traditional combination and the mixture works really well. In northern Spain, they use a bacon similar to the French lardon called tocino or scraps of Serrano ham. The sherry vinegar perfectly cuts the richness of both the scallops and bacon. Scallops should be served rare, so don't be tempted to cook them for long. Serve with some salad or sautéed potatoes.

8 large scallops

2 tablespoons extra virgin olive oil

2½ ounces bacon, or 4 slices

1 garlic clove, chopped

1 level tablespoon chopped rosemary

2 tablespoons sherry vinegar or dry sherry

Sea salt and freshly ground black pepper

Trim the hard white muscle from the side of the scallops and rinse them in cold water, then drain well and place on paper towels. Remove the coral or orange roe if you prefer, but this is not traditional in Europe.

Heat the olive oil in a large skillet to medium-hot and chop the bacon. Add to the pan and cook until nearly brown; it will carry on cooking a little, but don't remove it as the fat from the bacon flavors the scallops as they cook. Push the bacon to the side and add the scallops. Cook quickly, increasing the heat if need be, for only 1 minute per side.

Chop the garlic and add with the rosemary when you turn the scallops over. Mix in with the bacon. Season with salt and pepper and when the scallops are browned on both sides, add the sherry vinegar and remove from the heat. Toss the scallops and bacon in the sauce. Serve immediately.

roast cod with tomatoes, capers and olives

SERVES 2
PREPARATION TIME 5 MINUTES COOKING TIME 20–25 MINUTES

I had this dish in a restaurant by the sea in Corsica, and it seemed perfect for transportation back home. The trick was to have an ovenproof gratin dish, so you can start the cooking off on the top of the stove, then transfer it to the oven and quickly roast. You can, though, use a skillet and transfer everything to an ovenproof dish, but it must be preheated. Yellow bell peppers are a good contrast to the tomatoes, but red are fine too.

1 medium red onion

1 small yellow or red bell pepper

3 tablespoons extra virgin olive oil

1 tablespoon capers, in salt or brine

12 good quality black olives

1 level tablespoon rosemary

1 teaspoon fennel seeds (optional)

2 garlic cloves

6 ounces ripe tomatoes

1/2 large red chili, chopped (optional)

4 tablespoons red wine

2 cod steaks (about 8 ounces each)

Sea salt and freshly ground black pepper

Preheat the oven to 400°F and put in a gratin dish to heat if you don't have one that will cook on the burner. Heat a cast-iron gratin dish on the stove, or use a skillet.

Halve the onion and slice. Core and seed the pepper and cut into strips. Pour the olive oil into the gratin dish or skillet and cook the onion and pepper, turning the heat to low. Stir frequently at first to prevent the onion and pepper browning. Cook for about 15 minutes in total.

Meanwhile, rinse the capers, pit the olives, chop the rosemary, lightly crush the fennel seeds (if using), and slice the garlic.

Chop the tomatoes into 1/2-inch cubes, then add to the onion mixture with the garlic and chili, if using. Stir, then season with salt and pepper. Finally add the capers, olives, rosemary, and fennel seeds (if using), stir briefly and push to the side. Pour in the wine and remove from the heat.

Place the two steaks in the middle of the dish or pan (or transfer everything to the preheated gratin dish), season with salt and pepper, and put in the oven for about 10 minutes, until the cod is just cooked. Serve immediately or at room temperature.

poached salmon with sorrel

SERVES 4
PREPARATION TIME 5 MINUTES COOKING TIME 15 MINUTES

Sorrel is a very French ingredient and very easy to grow and cook. It is mostly available in the spring and summer months and has a distinct tart flavor. It is often served with fishcakes or salmon fillets. You can substitute some or all of the sorrel with spinach because sorrel does make a murky rather than a bright green sauce. The sauce can be prepared in advance; just reheat it, briefly and gently. Serve with Puy lentils or boiled potatoes.

4 x 5-ounce salmon fillets, skinned

1 small shallot

½ cup white wine

3½ ounces sorrel or selection of fresh herbs and spinach

2 tablespoons cold unsalted butter

4 tablespoons heavy cream

Pinch of freshly grated nutmeg

Sea salt and freshly ground black pepper

Ask your fishmonger to skin the salmon or run a sharp knife under the skin to remove.

Finely chop the shallot, or grate it on a fine grater. Put the wine, shallot, and 4 tablespoons water into a lidded sauté pan or saucepan large enough to accommodate the fish. Place the salmon fillets on top, season with salt and pepper, cover the pan, and bring to a gentle simmer. Cook the fish for about 5–10 minutes, until just cooked. The fish is half steamed, rather than being fully immersed in wine.

Meanwhile finely chop the sorrel, removing any tough stalks, and cube the butter and chill it in the fridge.

When the fish is cooked, remove carefully with a metal spatula (a sauté pan makes this easier), reserving the wine and shallots. Place on warm plates or on a serving dish, scraping off any bits of shallot that stick to them.

Bring the pan of wine and shallots to a boil, adding a little more water if the liquid has all reduced from cooking the fish, or reducing the wine if necessary—you need about 2 tablespoons of liquid. Add the butter and sorrel to the saucepan and cook them until the butter has melted and the sorrel wilted. Add the heavy cream, bring to a boil, and cook for 1 minute longer until you have a thin sauce. If you have a hand-held blender, you can whizz the sauce to amalgamate, but it's not essential.

Taste the sauce to correct the seasoning, adding a little salt, pepper, and freshly grated nutmeg. Pour over the fish and serve immediately.

how to cook a lobster

SERVES 2
PREPARATION TIME 2 MINUTES COOKING TIME 20–30 MINUTES

I've included a recipe for lobster as it is actually very easy to cook, and a stylish treat once you have found a good source for live ones. I think the best lobster is cooked at home, having first bought it live from a good fishmongers or local fisherman. There is more theory than practical hence the long intro. Lobster is such rich meat, that a generous squeeze of lemon juice and good-quality extra virgin olive oil drizzled over it is really all that you need as a sauce.

Lobsters are often served around the Mediterranean, mostly in restaurants catering for tourists with spare cash in their pockets! I've had many an argument about which is better: the coldwater lobster with large pincers which you find on the north-east coast of America and in England, or the Mediterranean variety which doesn't have the large pincers and consequently is often called spiny lobster. But as location counts for so much with eating, I'd prefer fresh spiny lobster on a hot sunny day in the Med!

Lobster has to be bought live. And by 'live' I mean active, not half starved and dead. It should move if prodded and not seem half asleep. Dealing with a live lobster is what puts most people off. The easiest, less traumatic way (for both lobster and cook) is to boil it, but placing it in cold water and slowly bringing up to a boil. This way the lobster goes to sleep as the water warms up and dies not slowly but peacefully. Which to me means it's been less traumatized. I also find the meat less chewy this way.

To extract the meat, you need a sharp knife (one that you don't mind blunting against the hard shell), a hammer, and pliers. You can have fancy lobster picks and a mallet, but in my experience a good-quality lobster is not necessarily near a well-stocked kitchen. As lobsters tend to spurt out juice when you smash the shell, wear an apron and, if possible, work outside to protect the kitchen.

I have suggested a 1½-pound lobster is enough for 2. I leave it up to you: if you feel up to eating more, buy two small (1 pound) lobsters.

1½-pound live lobster

Bay leaf (optional)

Dash of wine (optional)

Few peppercorns (optional)

to serve

Good quality extra virgin olive oil

Lemon wedges

Place the lobster into a saucepan large enough to accommodate it snugly and cover with cold water with a bay leaf, dash of wine and a few peppercorns if you wish. Cover with a lid and bring to a gentle boil. Once simmering, remove from the heat, then lift out the lobster to drain, then leave to cool (you can serve it either hot or cold).

Place the lobster on a board. With a sharp heavy knife, plunge down the middle of the back and through the body, heading towards the tail. Once you have made the initial stab through the shell, it isn't difficult to cut through it completely, but use one hand to steady the lobster so that it doesn't slip off the board. Cut the rest of the head in half. Allow half a lobster, on the shell, per person.

If the lobster has large pincers or claws, then carefully break the shell, pry open and remove the claw meat if possible in one. Or let your guests do the picking.

Serve with a drizzle of oil and lemon wedges for squeezing. A simple salad and boiled potatoes partner this well.

STYLISH MEDITERRANEAN IN MINUTES

sea bass baked in salt

SERVES 4
PREPARATION TIME 10 MINUTES COOKING TIME 20 MINUTES

A simple but delicious way to cook sea bass or similar round fish. If baking a larger fish, allow a little longer. If you are nervous about knowing when it's cooked, you can always break the salt to check and put it back in the oven if it's not ready—this will not affect the result. This is a splendid dish to present to the table and the fish is steamed beautifully.

2 x 1³/4-pound sea bass, scaled and gutted

Selection of herbs to stuff the fish

3 slices of lemon or lime

4 pounds fine sea salt

3 egg whites

to serve

Drizzle of extra virgin olive oil

Lemon wedges

Make sure the fish are well cleaned and dry. Place some herbs and the slices of lemon or lime in the cavity of the fish.

Preheat the oven to 400°F. Select a roasting pan or gratin dish into which the fish will fit snugly, ideally one with high sides. Pour the salt into the pan and add the egg whites. Mix the salt with the whites to create a damp moist mixture. Using about half the salt, pat down a base layer of salt. Put the fish on top and place the remaining salt around the fish, patting and sealing them all over. (It's a bit like covering your feet in the sand!) Add more salt if they are not completely covered.

Place the fish in the oven and roast for 20 minutes. Remove the fish from the oven and ideally leave to rest for 5 minutes. Do not leave the fish to rest much longer without breaking the salt crust to release the steam, otherwise the fish might be overcooked.

Carefully remove the salt crust and the skin from the fish (it will be too salty to eat) and use a large spatuala to transfer the flesh onto plates. Serve with a drizzle of oil and lemon wedges for squeezing.

meat and poultry

This chapter was possibly one of the hardest to compile when I first started thinking about what to include, keeping within my 30-minute rule. I had to ignore the many slow-cooked meat dishes that are so popular in the Mediterranean. No casseroles from France. No tagines from Morocco, no slow-cooked lamb so tender it falls off the bone from the Lebanon, and nothing cooked "al forno" from Italy. What we do have, though, are the easy grills, ground meats, and skewered kabobs that take far less time to prepare and cook. I didn't include the time it takes to light the barbecue but this is a natural choice for cooking meat if you can factor in getting the coals really hot. If not, or the weather really isn't favorable, a good broiler or cast-iron griddle on the burner is perfectly acceptable.

All parts of the animal are utilized. Nothing is wasted. Offal makes regular appearances on Mediterranean menus and deservedly so. A good piece of liver or pan-fried kidney is easy to cook and delicious, marrying well with rich or strong flavors such as mustard or sage.

Poultry, of course, can be cooked quickly and pigeon and quail, in common with the many game birds, is often served pink. Poaching chicken in broth is an ideal method of cooking when you're in a hurry but boned chicken, or chicken thighs or pieces, can be griddled or roasted fast.

lamb and pistachio kabobs

SERVES 4, MAKES ABOUT 16 KABOBS
PREPARATION TIME 15 MINUTES COOKING TIME 15 MINUTES

Kefta are spiced meatballs or kabobs. You will find them in the street markets of Morocco, Algeria, and throughout the Middle East. They make great barbecue food and you can prepare the kabobs in advance and keep them in the fridge until ready to cook. If you have any of the meat mixture left over, you can use it to make Moroccan briks (see page 87).

2 heaped teaspoons cumin seeds

2 garlic cloves, smashed with a little salt

1³/4 ounces pistachios

2 heaped tablespoons coarsely chopped flatleaf parsley or mint leaves

1¹/3 pounds ground lamb, preferably free-range

¹/2 large chili, finely chopped (optional)

1 ounce breadcrumbs (about 1 slice)

2 heaped teaspoons ground allspice

Sea salt and freshly ground black pepper

About 16 wooden skewers, soaked in water for about 10 minutes, or metal skewers

Preheat a barbecue, if using.

Grind the cumin seeds with the garlic into a paste using a mortar and pestle then add the nuts and coarsely grind. Alternatively, grind the cumin seeds in a spice grinder and finely chop the garlic and nuts. Coarsely chop the parsley, then mix the remaining ingredients together, seasoning well with salt and pepper.

Preheat a griddle, if using, to medium-hot.

Take a small ball of the lamb mixture (about 1³/4 ounces) and press around the top of a skewer so that it looks a cross between a lollypop and a cypress tree and is about 4 inches long. Press the mixture as firmly together as possible so the kabobs don't break up when cooking. Repeat with the rest of the mixture. Place the kabobs on a plate or tray ready for cooking.

When the griddle or barbecue is hot enough, place the kabobs on the grill and cook for about 10–15 minutes, turning over about 3 times to cook on all sides. To make sure the kabobs are cooked, break off a small amount of one kabob to check if the meat is cooked through. But lamb can be eaten slightly pink.

Serve with salad or remove the kabobs from their skewers and serve in pita bread.

Tip: Soaking the skewers in water prevents them from burning so quickly when broiling. Traditionally metal ones are used in many Mediterranean restaurants.

poussin with lemon and herbs

SERVES 4
PREPARATION TIME 5 MINUTES COOKING TIME 25 MINUTES

Poussins (baby chickens) are best here. If you can get them, ask your butcher to bone and butterfly them for you. Otherwise, chicken breasts or chicken thighs work just as well. Do buy them with the skin on because the stuffing goes under the skin. I like to use a mild soft goat cheese to make a creamier filling that oozes out during cooking to make a delicious sauce.

---

1 ounce each of marjoram or oregano, flatleaf parsley, mint, and basil

2 small garlic cloves

Zest and juice of 1 large lemon

5 ounces mild goat cheese (optional)

Extra virgin olive oil for cooking

2 poussins, boned, or 8 chicken thighs with skin on

Sea salt and freshly ground black pepper

Preheat the oven to 375°F and put in a baking sheet unless you have an ovenproof skillet.

Pick the leaves off the herbs and finely chop with a sharp knife. Smash the garlic with a little salt and zest the lemon (you need the juice for serving). Mix the herbs with the garlic, lemon zest, goat cheese, if using, and season with salt and pepper. Alternatively, place the herbs, garlic, lemon zest, salt and pepper in a food processor and blend until just chopped. Mix the cheese, if using, briefly in afterwards with the chopped herbs. Check the seasoning.

Stuff the herb mixture under the skin of each poussin or chicken thigh, loosening the skin from the flesh to create a pocket for the filling. (For chicken pieces I loosely divide the mixture into 8 to give myself an idea of how much mixture to stuff into each one.)

Heat a large ovenproof skillet and smear with a little olive oil. Place the chicken, skin-side down, into the pan and cook until the skin is golden brown (you may need to work in batches if using thighs). Season with salt and pepper and turn over, cooking for about 5 minutes on each side.

Once both sides are nicely brown, place the pan in the oven for another 15–20 minutes (or transfer everything to the preheated tray).

Remove the pan from the oven, being careful as the handle will be hot, and squeeze over a little lemon juice. Allow the chicken to rest for at least 5 minutes before serving.

roast quail stuffed with feta, figs, and pinenuts

SERVES 2–4
PREPARATION TIME 15 MINUTES COOKING TIME 10–15 MINUTES

I find one quail is plenty for me especially if it is stuffed and served with the Syrian Rice with Spinach and Dates on page 65. Alternatively, serve with Basmati rice cooked with a pinch of saffron for great color and braised spinach.

4 quail

3–4 tablespoons brandy

Sea salt and freshly ground black pepper

for the stuffing

1 small onion

4 tablespoons extra virgin olive oil

1 ounce pinenuts

2 garlic cloves

1 tablespoon chopped thyme or rosemary leaves

2½ ounces dried figs, finely chopped

1 ounce raisins or currants

3½ ounces feta

4 cocktail sticks or string

Preheat the oven to 400°F and put in a roasting pan or gratin dish into which the birds fit snugly—unless you have an ovenproof sauté pan.

Heat a lidded sauté pan or skillet to medium. Chop the onion and add 3 tablespoons of the oil to the pan and cook the onion and pinenuts in the oil for about 5 minutes to soften and lightly brown. Cover the pan to speed up the process. Chop the garlic, thyme, and figs then add to the pan along with the raisins and another tablespoon of oil. Cook gently for a few more minutes.

Remove the pan from the heat and crumble in the feta. Season with salt and pepper and stir the mixture well to incorporate all the ingredients. The stuffing can be made in advance and left in the fridge.

Briefly rinse the sauté pan and return to a medium-high heat. Divide the stuffing between the quail and stuff inside the cavity. Pierce the skin of the quail on either side of the stuffing end with a cocktail stick to partially seal in the stuffing. Pour 2 more tablespoons of olive oil into the sauté pan and seal the birds on all sides. (If you have time, wrapping a piece of string around the legs makes it easier to turn round, but it's not essential.)

When the quail are lightly browned, remove the pan from the heat and add the brandy. Place the pan in the oven or transfer everything to the hot roasting pan and cook for 10 minutes. I like my quail a little pink, so cook a little longer if you prefer.

If possible rest the birds for 5 minutes before serving.

chicken sautéed with orange and cardamom

SERVES 4
PREPARATION TIME 10 MINUTES COOKING TIME 20 MINUTES

This dish is inspired by an Israeli friend of mine. Jaffa, a name everyone associates with oranges, is a port in Israel from where oranges were exported. They are much used in Israeli cooking. It's a good combination: the tang of the orange cuts the fat of the chicken and the cardamom adds an exotic perfume. If your cardamom has sat unused in the cupboard for a good while, increase the amount here—or replace your supply! I got my butcher to prepare butterflied chicken for me as it takes too long for our purposes to bone it yourself. You might mention it's for pan-frying, not stuffing, so the bird can be cut in half: there's no need to keep all the skin intact for this recipe. If you can't get a whole boned chicken, use boned chicken breasts and thighs instead.

1 tablespoon extra virgin olive oil

1 small chicken, boned (about 1³/₄ pounds boned weight), or

4 boneless breasts or thighs

2 garlic cloves

Zest and juice of 1 large orange

12 cardamom pods

2 tablespoons chopped cilantro leaves (optional) to serve

Preheat the oven to 400°F and put in a gratin dish unless you have an ovenproof sauté pan or skillet.

Heat the oil in a large sauté pan or skillet. Add the chicken to the pan and cook on a medium high heat to brown. Turn over to brown on all sides, then put the pan in the oven or transfer everything to the hot gratin dish.

While the chicken is in the oven, chop the garlic, zest and juice the orange, and lightly crush the cardamom pods to remove the seeds then discard the pods. Lightly crush the seeds to release their perfume.

Remove the chicken from the oven after about 15 minutes. Make sure you cover the handle of the pan with a cloth as it will be very hot and move the chicken to the side. Add the garlic, mixing it into the oil to lightly cook. Add the cardamom, orange zest and juice, turn the chicken over in the pan to coat all sides with the juices and cook on the burner for about 1 minute to reduce the juices a little.

Serve immediately, sprinkled with cilantro if you wish. Delicious with boiled rice or the Rice, Lentils and Spices recipe on page 68.

pigeon with pomegranate sauce

SERVES 2
PREPARATION TIME 15 MINUTES COOKING TIME 10–15 MINUTES

This is a Syrian dish based on the same concept as the French duck with orange. The pomegranate syrup, which is quite sharp, works in the same way as orange juice, cutting the richness of the game. Pomegranate syrup is made from reducing the juice from pomegranates—you'll find it in bottles in most Middle Eastern stores or supermarkets that broth more unusual ingredients. Spatchcocking the pigeon is not difficult and it allows it to be broiled or roasted more easily within the time.

2 pigeon

2 tablespoons extra virgin olive oil

1 small red onion

1³/4 ounces walnut pieces (or halves broken into pieces)

2 tablespoons pomegranate syrup

4 tablespoons water

2 heaped teaspoons sugar

Sea salt and freshly ground black pepper

Preheat the oven to 350°F. The easiest way to cook this dish is in an ovenproof skillet or sauté pan. Alternatively preheat a small roasting pan or gratin dish into which the pigeon fit snugly.

To spatchcock the birds you need to remove the backbone first. Place the pigeon, breast-side down, on a board. Insert a pair of sharp scissors down the backbone, working from the leg end toward the neck. Cut along both sides of the backbone—it will come out as a long thin rectangle. Turn the pigeon over and press down so that it sits as flat as possible. Do the same with the second bird.

Heat a lidded skillet to medium-hot, add the olive oil, and brown the pigeons on all sides. Remove the birds and set aside.

While the pigeon is browning, quarter the onion then slice. Add the onion to the pan with the walnuts. Turn the heat to low, cover with a lid and gently cook for 5 minutes, until the onion is soft. Pour over the pomegranate syrup and the water and stir to dissolve the sugar into the juices. Season with salt and pepper and return the pigeon to the pan. Turn the pigeons on their breasts to coat in the juices.

Place the pan in the oven, or transfer everything to the preheated ovenproof dish and cook in the oven for 10 minutes if you like your meat on the pink side, or cook for another 5 minutes if you prefer. Check after 10 minutes and add a little more water if the juices have reduced too much.

Delicious served with Pumpkin with Chili and Nutmeg (see page 96) or Syrian Rice with Spinach and Dates (see page 65).

pan-fried kidneys with bacon and mustard

SERVES 4 AS AN APPETIZER OR 2–3 AS A MAIN COURSE
PREPARATION TIME 10 MINUTES COOKING TIME 10 MINUTES

Offal is not so popular today, but it often takes very little time to cook and is very much part of Mediterranean cooking as they will always use every part of the animal. Lamb's or calves' kidneys can be used, pig's is a bit tougher and stronger in flavor.

$^3/_4$ ounce dried porcini

14 ounces lamb's or calf's kidneys

$1^3/_4$ ounces smoked bacon

1 tablespoon chopped thyme or rosemary leaves

1 garlic clove

2 tablespoons butter

1 tablespoon olive oil

2 tablespoons brandy

4 tablespoons heavy cream

2 teaspoons good-quality wholegrain mustard

Sea salt and freshly ground black pepper

1 tablespoon coarsely chopped flatleaf parsley to garnish

Immerse the porcini in just enough hot water to cover them (too much water results in overcooking later) and set aside to soften. Halve the kidneys lengthways, remove the thin membrane on the outside if necessary and cut out the white fatty core. Cut into $^1/_2$-inch cubes and set aside. Dice the bacon or cut into strips. Chop the thyme and garlic and set aside.

Select a large skillet and heat up the oil and butter. When hot add the kidneys, cooking one side until just brown, then turning to brown the other side. Season with salt and pepper and remove carefully with a slotted spoon, keeping the butter and oil in the pan. Add the bacon and cook briefly.

Squeeze out the porcini, reserving the soaking liquid, and add to the pan along with the garlic and thyme. Cook, stirring frequently, until the bacon is just lightly browned. Return the kidneys to the pan along with the reserved porcini liquid, discarding any sediment at the bottom of the bowl. Then add the brandy. Cook for a few minutes to reduce the liquid until it makes a thick sauce. Add the cream and mustard, bring to a boil, and when the sauce just coats the kidneys, remove from the heat.

Taste to check the seasoning and serve immediately with a scattering of parsley, either on thin crispy toast, with a small warm brioche or with boiled rice.

calf's liver with marsala and sage

SERVES 2
PREPARATION TIME 5 MINUTES, COOKING TIME 5 MINUTES

Mediterranean cooks use every part of the animal and the liver is probably the most popular of all offal. Many believe the most prized to be calf's liver. But you can use chicken livers or possibly lamb's liver too. This dish is delicious with Pumpkin with Chili and Nutmeg (see page 96). Italians would also serve polenta as well and Venetians often serve it with slow-cooked onions because their sweetness complements the liver.

If you like your liver pink, then make sure it isn't sliced too thinly, otherwise it will overcook before it has a chance to seal on the outside.

2 tablespoons extra virgin olive oil

8 large sage leaves

10 ounces calf's liver, or 2 slices

1 large garlic clove, sliced

3 tablespoons Marsala or sweet sherry

3 tablespoons heavy cream (optional)

Sea salt and freshly ground black pepper

Prepare and measure all the ingredients before cooking, as the liver takes very little time to cook. Have your accompanying vegetables ready too.

Pour the olive oil into a large skillet and heat to high. Add 4 sage leaves and quickly fry until just crisp. Set aside.

Add the liver to the pan, season with salt and pepper and turn over, cooking for about 1–2 minutes, depending on how you like your liver cooked, until golden brown on both sides. Remove the liver to a hot plate and add the garlic and remaining sage leaves. Cook briefly then add the Marsala, and remove from the heat as it starts to sizzle and reduce. Stir in the cream (if using). Pour the Marsala mixture over the liver and serve with the reserved crispy sage leaves as a garnish.

lamb marinated in yogurt and spices

SERVES 6
PREPARATION TIME 5 MINUTES COOKING TIME 20 MINUTES
MARINATING TIME UP TO 12 HOURS

I have used neck of lamb for this recipe, but a boned and butterflied leg of lamb would be a good party substitute. It could also be successfully cooked on the broiler. But allow the lamb to cook slowly to prevent the yogurt from burning too much. If you prefer, remove most of the yogurt marinade before barbecuing then add at the last minute. For more of a sauce, heat up the yogurt marinade in a saucepan separately with a teaspoon of cornstarch mixed with water to prevent it from separating. Alternatively, cube the neck of lamb and thread on kabob sticks, soaking the sticks in water first if they're wooden. Serve with saffron rice, couscous, or tabbouleh.

2 pounds trimmed neck of lamb (in the one piece, unless you are cooking as kabobs)

3/4 cup thick drained yogurt

2 garlic cloves, smashed with a little salt

2 teaspoons coriander seeds, dry-roasted and freshly ground

2 teaspoons cumin seeds, dry-roasted and freshly ground

1 level teaspoon allspice (optional)

Cilantro sprigs to garnish

Marinate the lamb in the yogurt, garlic, and spices. Ideally leave overnight or a minimum of 2 hours.

Preheat the grill to high or the oven to 400°F and put in a baking sheet to heat.

Lift the lamb and its marinade onto the pan, cover with foil, and broil or roast for about 20 minutes, depending on how thick the piece is. Turn the lamb half way through and, if you're broiling it and it is starting to burn, lower the temperature slightly. Once cooked through, remove and leave to rest for 5 minutes. Scatter with cilantro to serve.

poached chicken with egg, tarragon, and caper sauce

SERVES 4
PREPARATION TIME 10 MINUTES COOKING TIME 15 MINUTES

Poaching a chicken is classic home cooking. At least two meals prepared at once. The chicken is cooked while simultaneously providing broth for another meal—and you could cook some vegetables in the broth to serve with the chicken.

I've enjoyed this dish in France as well as Italy, flavored with either tarragon or parsley. But you could probably find this features in most home cooking throughout the Mediterranean. The pinenuts give the sauce a rich nutty flavor. Almonds can be substituted or you can omit the nuts altogether. The bread might seem a strange addition, but it acts as a binding agent and absorbs the vinegar and oil, making the sauce more homogeneous. Of course, you can also broil the chicken but traditionally this sauce is served with poached chicken.

4 chicken breasts (about 1¼ pounds)

6 peppercorns

1 bayleaf (optional)

Sprig of fresh herbs (or leftover stalks)

2 garlic cloves

for the egg and caper sauce

1 ounce pinenuts

2 eggs

1 small slice bread or 2 heaped tablespoons fresh breadcrumbs (½ ounce)

1 tablespoon capers

2 heaped tablespoons coarsely chopped fresh tarragon or flatleaf parsley

2 level teaspoons French mustard

1 tablespoon red wine vinegar

4 tablespoons good quality extra virgin olive oil

Preheat the oven to 400°F.

Put the pinenuts in the oven and lightly brown for about 5–10 minutes. (Use a timer, so you don't forget them as they burn easily.) When done, remove and chop. Set aside.

Place the chicken in a large lidded saucepan and add the peppercorns, bayleaf, herbs, and garlic. Bring just to a boil and simmer gently with the lid half on for about 10 minutes. Set aside and remove from the broth if you wish to serve the chicken at room temperature, otherwise, leave in the broth until you serve.

As soon as you have put the chicken in the pan, carefully place the eggs in another pan, bring to a boil and cook for 10 minutes. Rinse under cold water for a minute, peel, finely chop, and set aside.

Meanwhile, put the bread in a small bowl and lightly soak in a little water to soften. Rinse the capers, squeeze dry, and coarsely chop. Place the capers in another bowl and add the pinenuts, chopped egg, tarragon, mustard, vinegar, and olive oil. Squeeze the bread, to remove any excess water and add, mixing all the ingredients together properly.

Strain the broth and leave to cool, then refrigerate. Remove any fat that has congealed on top and use for another recipe.

Serve with boiled or steamed vegetables, such as carrots, onions and celery, or with a green salad.

broiled steak with anchovy butter

SERVES 4
PREPARATION TIME 10 MINUTES COOKING TIME 2–10 MINUTES
(DEPENDING ON HOW YOU LIKE YOUR MEAT COOKED)

Anchovies in the Mediterranean are more like a salty seasoning than fish. They are salted to preserve them and these are the type you need for this recipe. In France they use butter on the steak; in Italy they would use olive oil. I prefer to follow the French here, as the butter slowly melts over the steak like a sauce. I chose tarragon as my herb, as it works very well with steak, but rosemary is more Italian and can be substituted. This sauce works just as well with lamb chops, salmon, or a firm white fish. It can be prepared in advance and keeps in the fridge for at least a week if well sealed. Do buy your steak from a reputable butcher, ideally well hung for a better flavor. Unwrap it if it is covered in plastic wrap so it doesn't sweat and keep it in the fridge or a cool place.

---

1 garlic clove

1 ounce salted anchovies in olive oil (1³/₄-ounce can)

1 tablespoon chopped tarragon leaves

1 tablespoon lemon juice

¹/₂ stick unsalted butter

4 x 7-ounce good quality steaks, rump or sirloin

Olive oil for greasing

1 red onion

Lemon wedges to serve (optional)

Sea salt and freshly ground black pepper

Preheat a griddle to medium-hot or prepare a barbecue if you have time. Remove the steak from the fridge 15 minutes before you want to cook so the meat is not too cold. The shock of hitting the heat is less extreme and this encourages tenderness.

Make the anchovy sauce first. Purée the garlic and anchovies using a mortar and pestle or, if possible, the small bowl of a food processor for best and quickest results. Scrape down the sides of the bowl so the ingredients chop evenly. Add freshly ground pepper, the tarragon, and lemon juice and purée again. Slowly add the butter, small amounts at a time, and mix until it is homogeneous. Taste for seasoning and chill in the freezer until the steaks are cooked. This stage can be done in advance.

Season the steak with salt and pepper, then very lightly grease with olive oil to prevent too many flames appearing, and cook the meat over a fierce heat on both sides to your preferred consistency, ideally rare or medium rare. Slice the onion into thick rings then cook them around the meat, turning once.

Remove from the griddle and serve on a plate with a dollop of anchovy butter and a wedge of lemon, if using. Normally the steak is too large to serve with anything else on the plate. A simple salad and country bread or a few potatoes, roasted or fried, are perfect accompaniments.

pork tenderloin with pears and sweet sherry

SERVES 4 AS TAPAS OR 2 AS A MAIN COURSE
PREPARATION TIME 10 MINUTES COOKING TIME 20 MINUTES

I was fortunate enough to go to a tapas festival when I was last in Spain. Before the sherry tasting got to me, I managed to sample some delicious tapas. This was one of them. The quality of the sherry really makes this dish. You can also use an even sweeter Spanish dessert wine made from the Pedro Ximenez grape, or Marsala, dessert wine from Sicily. But sweet sherry can be used in a variety of recipes, so a bottle won't be wasted. Pork tenderloin is the small fillet rather than the larger loin of pork. It cooks quickly and small slices of meat work well as tapas.

1 pound pork tenderloin

2 tablespoons extra virgin olive oil

1 small red onion

2 garlic cloves

1 pear, not too hard if possible

scant ½ cup sweet oloroso sherry

Few tablespoons chicken broth (optional)

Sea salt and freshly ground black pepper

Heat a lidded sauté pan to medium-hot. (The trick to pan-frying meat is the temperature of the pan. It should be hot enough to brown and seal the meat, but not so hot that you burn the bottom of the pan, as the sediment left adds a delicious flavor to the final sauce.)

Trim the tenderloin of any white sinew and cut into ½-inch slices. Add the oil to the pan and when hot add the pork. Cook the slices, browning on both sides. Remove when the meat is sealed and brown, but if the slices are thicker, reduce the heat a little to cook through.

Meanwhile, chop the onion and slice the garlic.

Remove the meat to a bowl and add the onion and garlic to the pan. Cover the pan with the lid and gently cook the onion, scraping all the tasty sediment left by the meat (add a dash of water to help remove it before it burns if the pan is too hot).

While the onion is cooking, peel the pear, quarter, core, and cut into thin slices. Add the pear and continue to cook for another 5 minutes, covered. When the onion and pear are soft return the meat to the pan, mixing into the onions and season with salt and pepper.

Increase the heat to medium-hot, add the sherry and cook at a brisk simmer for 2 minutes to amalgamate the flavors. If you like your meat with a bit more sauce you can add a few tablespoons chicken broth or even water when the sauce comes to a boil.

Set aside for a few minutes then serve as a tapas or main course.

desserts

Something sweet to end a meal is, for most Mediterraneans, plain fresh fruit, sherbets, or ice creams. It's often far too hot to want anything heavy or too rich at the end of a meal and besides, delicious fruit grows everywhere! A big bowl of tasty fresh fruit, whatever is in season, always looks good. During the full heat of summer, fruit may be served immersed in a bowl of iced water to keep it cool and people help themselves while they sit and chat. Tree fruits, such as cherries, apricots, or peaches, work well but not raspberries or strawberries—they just get soggy.

Another reason why you don't find homemade desserts is because patisseries and bakers are an integral part of Mediterranean society, and it is very traditional to buy cake or delicious cookies to serve with a sweet wine or a digestive such as grappa or strong black coffee. Moroccans and Tunisians have lots of sweet little biscuits: why would people make them when they are so much easier and tastier to buy? Greeks have their mini lozenges of baklava—layers of wafer-thin pastry drenched in honey and nuts, and in Cyprus and Turkey you are offered lokum (Turkish delight). These sweet morsels work perfectly with the small dark shots of coffee that are served with them. In Italy, a typically easy and stylish way of ending a meal is to dunk some cantuccini cookies in vino santo, a dessert wine. And the Spanish have a wine called Pedro Ximenez which is delicious poured over some good-quality ice cream.

The recipes I give here in the main based on fruit, but none of them are overly rich or heavy: the perfect way to end a truly satisfying meal.

apple fritters

baked figs

SERVES 4

PREPARATION TIME 10 MINUTES   COOKING TIME 20 MINUTES

Simple, delicious, and indulgent! Try with a shot of grappa, brandy, or other digestive.

for the batter

½ cup plus 2 tablespoons plain flour

2 heaped teaspoons caster or vanilla sugar

½ teaspoon cinnamon powder

Pinch of salt

1 egg

⅓ cup plus 1 tablespoon water

1 teaspoon sunflower oil

1 cup sunflower oil

4 eating apples (about 1 pound)

Confectioners' sugar for dusting

Place the flour into a bowl. Add the sugar, cinnamon, and salt and mix. Break the egg into another bowl and mix with the water. Make a well in the middle of the flour and add the egg mixture. Slowly mix together, bringing the flour gently into the egg mixture to prevent too many lumps, using a small whisk if possible or a wooden spoon. Stir in the sunflower oil and add a little water if the batter is too gluey, but it should be a thick cream consistency. Set aside to rest.

Gently heat the sunflower oil in a large skillet. Peel the apples and slice on the equator, into disks about finger-width thick. Tap out any seeds, but the core will soften when cooked. Increase the heat of the pan to medium high. Place a few apple disks in the batter to coat both sides. Lifting the bowl over the skillet, add the apples, one at a time, to prevent drips on the side. Cook in batches for about 2–3 minutes on each side. Drain on paper towels, allow to cool for a few minutes, then sprinkle with powdered sugar and serve immediately.

SERVES 4

PREPARATION TIME 5 MINUTES   COOKING TIME 20 MINUTES

Figs are plentiful throughout the Med, appearing at the end of summer and through fall. Delicious fresh, of course, but this Turkish dish works well for a more complex, stylish dessert.

Pat of butter for greasing the gratin dish

10 figs

⅓ cup brandy

1 tablespoon honey

Zest and juice of ½ lemon

1 ounce toasted pistachios or almonds, coarsely chopped (optional)

½ cup thick drained yogurt

Preheat the oven to 375°F.

Choose a gratin dish into which all the figs will fit snugly and grease it with the butter. Halve the figs and place in the dish. Pour the brandy over the figs and drizzle over the honey. Mix together the lemon zest, nuts (if using), and yogurt and spoon a dollop on each fig half. Drizzle the lemon juice around the figs and place in the oven.

Bake the figs for about 20 minutes until the juices have reduced into a syrup. If the figs look cooked but the juices are not reduced enough, pour the juices into a saucepan and reduce, keeping an eye on it at all times to prevent it burning.

Serve hot or at room temperature with extra yogurt if you wish.

sautéed peaches with almonds

SERVES 4
PREPARATION TIME 10 MINUTES COOKING TIME 10 MINUTES

A quick dessert that tastes delicious served with good-quality vanilla ice cream or whipped cream. I used only 3 medium-large peaches that were just ripe, calculating 6 wedges per person to be enough. That was also the amount that fitted snugly into my large skillet. You don't want peaches that are too hard, or they won't have developed any flavor, but not too soft either as they will be hard to peel and cut. I quartered the peaches to make them easier to remove from the pitt. If they are too soft, they might become very mushy when removing from pitt; don't worry if they break up a little, though. A little lemon juice squeezed over the cooked peaches just before serving cuts their sweetness. I used blanched almonds and toasted them, but if you are able to buy ready toasted, you save even more time.

1 ounce blanched almonds

3 medium-large peaches

1 ounce unsalted butter

½ tablespoon sugar

Pinch of cinnamon

2–3 tablespoons brandy (optional)

Squeeze of lemon juice

Spread out the nuts on a baking pan in the oven and switch it on to 400°F. Cook for about 10 minutes until golden brown, checking just beforehand if your oven heats up quickly. Remove from the oven and set aside.

Peel the peaches and score into quarters, lengthwise. Carefully remove the peach from the pitt and cut each quarter in halves, to make 8 wedges per peach.

Heat a large skillet to high. When it is really hot, toss in the butter and add the peaches, placing them all neatly on one cut side so that they cook evenly. The art here is to lightly brown the peaches without burning the butter too much and before the juice is released which makes it hard to brown.

Sprinkle over a little sugar and cinnamon and cook the peaches for about 5–10 minutes in total, gently turning over the slices when they are browned on one side.

Carefully pour in the brandy, if using, and lemon juice. Mix briefly by tilting and shaking the pan or by delicately turning the peaches over in the juices with a spatula, so the slices don't break up.

Remove from the heat and serve hot or at room temperature.

deep-fried pasta ribbons

SERVES 4
PREPARATION TIME 2 MINUTES COOKING TIME 15 MINUTES

This is a great way to use up leftover cooked tagliatelle or pappadelle. Because a good Italian mama would never waste any ingredient, they often deep-fry the remains for a little nibble with coffee or a simple dessert with a glass of grappa or coffee. This recipe calls for fresh egg pasta, not the dried variety.

3½ ounces egg pasta such as tagliatelle or pappadelle

2 cups sunflower oil

Confectioners' sugar

Bring a large saucepan of well-salted water to a boil. Drop in the fresh egg pasta into the water and cook for about 1 minute, or follow the instructions on the packet. Drain well and spread the strands on paper towels to dry and prevent them from sticking together.

Heat a wok or deep-sided skillet with the sunflower oil to medium-high and carefully add a few strands of pasta at a time to just cover the bottom of the pan. Curl them round as you put them in as they will come out rigid and cook for about 1 minute, turning over if need be.

Remove and drain on paper towels while you cook the rest. Sprinkle the strands generously with confectioners' sugar.

Serve with a glass of grappa or coffee.

caramelized blood oranges with marsala

SERVES 4–6
PREPARATION TIME 10 MINUTES COOKING TIME 10 MINUTES

If blood oranges are in season, then the color is great. But the recipe works just as successfully with ordinary ones. Marsala is a fortified dessert wine from the western tip of Sicily; grappa is the Italian name for a grape spirit they enjoy in coffee or as a digestive after meals.

6 large oranges

5 ounces sugar

⅓ cup water

1 ounce almonds, toasted

2 tablespoons marsala or grappa

Biscotti to serve

Remove the skin from the oranges, using a small serrated knife for easiest results. Cut off the top and base, stand each orange upright and carefully remove the pith from top to base so only the flesh of the orange is left.

Cut the orange into round disks, about a finger-width thick and remove any seeds. Arrange in a largish shallow bowl, overlapping slightly.

Half way through cutting the oranges, start the caramel as you'll need to keep a careful eye on it while it cooks. Place the sugar in a small saucepan with the water. Make sure you don't get too many sugar crystals around the sides as these will prevent the sugar from melting evenly and can burn before the sugar is properly cooked. Don't stir the sugar either, otherwise it will crystallize. Cook the sugar for 5–10 minutes until it has turned a golden caramel color and all the water has evaporated. Pour the syrup over the oranges in attractive drizzles rather than big lumps (or try making spun sugar—see right).

Coarsely chop the almonds and scatter over the oranges. Sprinkle over the Marsala or grappa. Serve with biscotti.

Spun sugar: You can also have fun making spun sugar, as shown in the photograph here. It's much easier to achieve than you might imagine. Once the sugar has cooked and the water evaporated, leave the sugar to cool down for about 5 minutes. As the sugar cools, it will start to form thin threads as it drops from the spoon. Spin this over the plate, and it will solidify as you scatter. The effect won't last for long, and humidity will make the strands collapse but it's a very stylish presentation!

Tip: You can leave the dish to marinate but I like to serve it immediately to get the crunchiness of the caramel—hence the importance of drizzling the caramel in thin strips, so that your teeth don't have to deal with large rock-hard lumps. But if you want it to marinate, especially in the fridge, the acidity of the oranges and humidity of the fridge melt the caramel into a sauce.

broiled sabayon with fruit

SERVES 4
PREPARATION TIME 5 MINUTES COOKING TIME 15 MINUTES

This easy dish can only be done at the last minute, but it's worth it! You can prepare and arrange the fruit ahead of cooking if you want. A variety of fruit can be used. The only rule is to choose fruit that is in season or just plain tasty.

8 heaped tablespoons fresh fruit, such as raspberries, cherries, and/or pineapple

1/3 cup kirsch, other fruit liqueur or Marsala

3 eggs

6 tablespoons sugar

Pinch of vanilla pod seeds, or 1 teaspoon vanilla extract

2 tablespoons unsalted butter

1 heaped tablespoon all-purpose flour

Prepare the fruit and arrange in individual gratin dishes or one large one about 9 inches x 10 inches. Drizzle the alcohol over the fruit to marinate. Preheat the broiler to medium-high.

Bring a small saucepan a quarter full of water to a boil. Put the eggs, sugar, and vanilla in a heatproof bowl over the pan and whisk until double in size, and light and fluffy. Use an electric whisk to save your arm, and cook for about 10 minutes. Make sure the water does not touch the bottom of the bowl. Keep whisking all the time the eggs are over the water, so they don't curdle. The eggs should be semi-cooked.

Remove the bowl from the pan and discard the water. Melt the butter in the pan. Pour 1 tablespoon of the alcohol from the marinating fruit into the egg mixture, then add the melted butter. Sift in the flour, and lightly beat the mixture until just incorporated.

Spoon the sabayon over the prepared fruit. Place under the broiler, not too close to the element, and brown the sabayon for about 1–2 minutes. Watch carefully as the top can quickly burn. Serve immediately.

vanilla ice cream with marinated raisins and sherry

SERVES 4
PREPARATION TIME 2 MINUTES COOKING TIME 2 MINUTES
MARINATING TIME 20 MINUTES

I had a wonderful dessert in southern Spain, which consisted of raisins soaked in sweet sherry mixed into vanilla ice cream with more sherry poured on top. The Italians have the same concept of pouring alcohol or coffee over vanilla ice cream. The heat of the coffee or the vapors of the alcohol, work wonderfully with the ice cream. And it's a great way of making bought ice cream a little more special. Use a good-quality sweet sherry or Pedro Ximenez wine for this dessert, but Marsala or grappa would be good substitutes. Most Spanish markets have wonderfully fat raisins: look out for good-quality ones. And do buy decent ice cream!

5 ounces raisins such as large plump Muscavo raisins

2 heaped teaspoons sugar

2/3 cup sweet oloroso sherry

4 large scoops good-quality vanilla ice cream

Put the raisins in a small saucepan and add the sugar and sherry. Bring to a gentle boil and simmer briefly for about 2 minutes maximum. Set aside, placing in a bowl so they cool down more quickly.

Put the scoops of ice cream in a bowl and pour over the fruit and alcohol. Serve immediately.

index

Aioli, saffron 45
anchovies 8
antipasti *see* snacks and appetizers
Apple fritters 150
Artichokes, deep-fried 95
Asparagus, broiled 92

Baba ganoush (eggplant purée) 12
Baked figs 150
Baked red mullet with grape leaves 106
Baked sea bream with fennel and chili 110
Baked mushrooms with proscuitto
  and goats' cheese 84
basmati rice 61
Beet, green bean and preserved
  lemon salad 48
Blood oranges with marsala, caramelized 157
Borlotti and green bean salad 55
bottarga 8, 75, 83
bouillabaisse 33
Braised cabbage with bacon and nutmeg 100
Braised radicchio and smoked
  mozzarella bruschetta 17
Braised zucchini with olives 100
bread 6, 7
Bread salad (fattoush) 52
Briks with eggs, fish or meat 87
Broiled eggplant with cilantro and chili 51
Broiled sabayon with fruit 158
Broiled seafood with chilies 111
Broiled steak with anchovy butter 144
Broiled swordfish with tapenade 117
bruschetta 15, 29
bulgar wheat, 20, 68
Bulgar wheat with chickpeas, pinenuts
  and currants 68

Cabbage with bacon and nutmeg, braised 100
Calf's liver with marsala and sage 142
Caramelized blood oranges with marsala 157
Carrot and tahini salad 29
Carrots with cumin 96
Cauliflower and carrots with cumin
  and cardamom, marinated 59
Chicken livers, spinach, currants
  and pinenuts on toast 29
Chicken sautéed with orange and cardamom 137
Chicken with egg, tarragon and

caper sauce, poached 143
Chickpea fritters 15
citrus fruits 8
Clam and lardon soup 34
Cod with tomatoes, capers and
  olives, roast 125
cracked wheat 68
Cucumber salad with pomegranates
  and mint 48

Deep-fried artichokes 95
Deep-fried zucchini salad with
  mint and chili 56
Deep-fried fish 121
Deep-fried pasta ribbons 154
Deep-fried sage leaves with
  anchovies 19
desserts
  Apple fritters 150
  Baked figs 150
  Broiled sabayon with fruit 158
  Caramelized blood oranges with marsala 157
  Deep-fried pasta ribbons 154
  Sautéed peaches with almonds 153
  Vanilla ice cream with marinated
    raisins and sherry 158
Dukkah 31

Eggplant purée, smoked 12
Eggplant, tomato and mint salad 51
Eggplant with cilantro and chili, broiled 51
Eggplant with feta, sesame seeds
  and paprika, pan-fried 88
Eggplant with sumac, roasted 99
Eggs with yogurt, chili and coriander 83
Eggs en cocotte 80

Fattoush (bread salad) 51
Fava beans with fresh cheese 80
Fennel and orange salad 56
Figs, baked 150
Feta and chickpea salad with
  peppers and cilantro 88
fish and seafood
  Baked red mullet with grape leaves 106
  Baked sea bream with fennel and chili 110
  Broiled seafood with chilies 111
  Broiled swordfish with tapenade 117

Clam and lardon soup 34
Deep-fried fish 121
Deep-fried sage leaves with anchovies 19
Fish patties 116
Frittata with bottarga and asparagus 83
How to cook a lobster 128
Leeks with caper, parsley and
  anchovy sauce 55
Marinated octopus salad 22
Mussels with curry 109
Pan-fried scallops with bacon and
  sherry vinegar 122
Pasta with anchovies, broiled
  peppers and pangritata 72
Pasta with clams 62
Pasta with zucchini, bottarga and
  lemon zest 75
Poached salmon with sorrel 126
Roast cod with tomatoes, capers
  and olives 125
Sardines with chermoula sauce 112
Sea bass stuffed with prunes and
  tamarind 115
Sea bass baked in salt 129
Shrimp, white bean and dill salad 66
Skate with caper and parsley sauce 118
Smoked eel and flageolet salad 77
Spanish fish soup with rice and saffron 40
Frittata with bottarga and asparagus 83
fruit
  Apple fritters 150
  Baked figs 150
  Broiled sabayon with fruit 158
  Bulgar wheat with chickpeas,
    pinenuts and currants 68
  Caramelized blood oranges with marsala 157
  Chicken livers, spinach, currants
    and pinenuts on toast 29
  Chicken sautéed with orange and
    cardamom 137
  Cucumber salad with
    pomegranates and mint 48
  Fennel and orange salad 56
  Pigeon with pomegranate sauce 139
  Pork tenderloin with pears and
    sweet sherry 147
  Prunes wrapped in bacon and
    stuffed with walnuts 26

Quail stuffed with feta, figs and pinenuts 136
Sautéed peaches with almonds 153
Sea bass stuffed with prunes and
  tamarind 115
Syrian rice with spinach and dates 65
Vanilla ice cream with marinated
  raisins and sherry 158

garlic mayonnaise (aioli) 45
Gazpacho 41
Green beans braised with tomatoes
  and basil 95

Harissa sauce 42
herbs 8
hors d'oeuvres *see* snacks and appetizers

Ice cream with marinated raisins and
  sherry, vanilla 158
Italian broccoli and broth soup 37

Kebabs, lamb and pistachio 133

Lamb and pistachio kebabs 133
Lamb marinated in yogurt and spices 142
Leeks with caper, parsley and
  anchovy sauce 55
legumes
  Borlotti and green bean salad 55
  Bulgar wheat with chickpeas,
    pinenuts and currants 68
  Chickpea fritters 15
  Fava beans with fresh cheese 80
  Feta and chickpea salad with
    peppers and cilantro 88
  Lima beans with chorizo 30
  Rice, lentils and spices 68
  Shrimp, white bean and dill salad 66
  Squid, chickpea and tomato soup 39
  Smoked eel and flageolet salad 77
  Spinach and chickpea stew 69
  Lentil salad with lardons and walnuts 74
Lentil salad with lardons and walnuts 74
Lima beans with chorizo 30
Lobster, how to cook 128

Marinated cauliflower and carrots
  with cumin and cardamom 59

Marinated octopus salad 22
meat *see also* poultry
  Baked mushrooms with prosciutto
    and goats' cheese 84
  Briks with eggs, fish or meat 87
  Calf's liver with marsala and sage 142
  Chicken livers, spinach, currants
    and pinenuts on toast 29
  Clam and lardon soup 34
  Grilled steak with anchovy butter 144
  Lamb and pistashio kebabs 133
  Lamb marinated in yogurt and spices 142
  Lentil salad with lardons and walnuts 74
  Lima beans with chorizo 30
  Pan-fried kidneys with bacon and mustard 140
  Pan-fried scallops with bacon and
    sherry vinegar 122
  Pork tenderloin with pears and
    sweet sherry 147
  Prunes wrapped in bacon and
    stuffed with walnuts 26
  Wilted spinach with Serrano ham and eggs 84
mezze *see* snacks and appetizers
Mozzarella and Parmesan fritters 15
mujadarra 68
Mushrooms with prosciutto and
  goats' cheese, baked 84
Mussels with curry 109

Octopus salad, marinated 22
olive oils 47

Pan-fried eggplant with feta, sesame
  seeds and paprika 88
Pan-fried kidneys with bacon and mustard 140
Pan-fried scallops with bacon and
  sherry vinegar 122
Pasta and squid ink sauce 71
Pasta ribbons, deep-fried 154
Pasta with anchovies, grilled peppers
  and pangritata 72
Pasta with clams 62
Pasta with zucchini, bottarga and lemon 75
Patatas bravas 103
Peaches with almonds, sautéed 153
Pigeon with pomegranate sauce 139
Poached chicken with egg, tarragon
  and caper sauce 143
Poached salmon with sorrel 126
pomegranate syrup 8
Pork tenderloin with pears and sherry 147
Poussin with lemon and herbs 134
poultry
  Chicken sautéed with orange and
    cardamom 137
  Poussin with lemon and herbs 134

Poached chicken with egg, tarragon
  and caper sauce 143
Pigeon with pomegranate sauce 139
Roast quail stuffed with feta, figs
  and pinenuts 136
Prunes wrapped in bacon and stuffed
  with walnuts 26
Pumpkin with chili and nutmeg 96

Quail stuffed with feta, figs and pinenuts, 136

rice 40, 61
Rice, lentils and spices 68
Rice with spinach and dates, Syrian 65
Roasted eggplant with sumac 99
Roast cod with tomatoes, capers and olives 125
Roast quail stuffed with feta, figs and
  pinenuts, 136
Romesco sauce 42

Sabayon with fruit, grilled 158
Saffron aioli 45
Saffron potatoes with red onions 103
Sage leaves with anchovies, deep-fried 19
salads
  Beet, green bean and preserved
    lemon salad 48
  Borlotti bean and green bean salad 55
  Broiled eggplant with cilantro and chili 51
  Carrot and tahini salad 29
  Cucumber salad with pomegranates
    and mint 48
  Deep-fried zucchini salad with mint
    and chili 56
  Eggplant, tomato and mint salad 51
  Fattoush (bread salad) 52
  Fennel and orange salad 56
  Feta and chickpea salad with peppers
    and cilantro 88
  Leeks with capers, parsley and
    anchovy sauce 55
  Lentil salad with lardons and walnuts 74
  Lima beans with fresh cheese 80
  Marinated cauliflower and carrots
    with cumin and cardamom 59
  Marinated octopus salad 22
  Shrimp, white bean and dill salad 66
  Smoked eel and flageolet salad 77
  Tabbouleh 20
Salmon with sorrel, poached 126
Salsa verde 45
Sardines with chermoula sauce 112
sauces
  Caper and parsley 118
  Caper, parsley and anchovy 55
  Chermoula 112

Egg, tarragon and caper 143
Harissa 42
Pomegranate 139
Romesco 42
Saffron aioli 45
Salsa verde 45
Tapenade 117
Sautéed peaches with almonds 153
Sautéed spring vegetables with yogurt
  and mint 99
Scallops with bacon and sherry vinegar 122
Sea bass baked in salt 129
Seafood with chilies, broiled 111
Skate with caper and parsley sauce 118
Shrimp, white bean and dill salad 66
Smoked eel and flageolet salad 77
soups
  clam and lardon soup 34
  Italian broccoli and broth soup 37
  Gazpacho 41
  Squid, chickpea and tomato soup 39
  Spinach, tarragon and yogurt soup 36
  Spanish fish soup with rice and saffron 40
snacks and appetizers
  Braised radicchio and smoked
    mozzarella bruschetta 17
  Carrot and tahini salad 29
  Chicken livers, spinach, currants and
    pinenuts on toast 29
  Chickpea fritters 15
  Deep-fried sage leaves with anchovies 19
  Dukkah 31
  Lima beans with chorizo 30
  Marinated octopus salad 22
  Mozzarella and Parmesan fritters 17
  Prunes wrapped in bacon and stuffed
    with walnuts 26
  Tabbouleh 20
  Tuna tartare with crème fraiche and chervil 15
  Smoked eggplant purée 12
  Vegetable platter 25
Spanish fish soup with rice and saffron 40
Spanish tomato bread with manchego
  and olives 20
Spinach and chickpea stew 69
Spinach, tarragon and yogurt soup 36
Spring vegetables with yogurt and mint 99
Squid, chickpea and tomato soup 39
Squid ink pasta sauce 71
Steak with anchovy butter, grilled 144
sumac 8
Swordfish with tapenade, grilled 117
Syrian rice with spinach and dates 65

Tabbouleh 20
tapas *see* snacks and appetizers

Tomato bread with manchego and olives 20
tamarind 8
Tuna tartare with crème fraîche and chervil 15

Vanilla ice cream with raisins and sherry 158
vegetables
  Beet, green bean and preserved lemon
    salad 48
  Borlotti bean and green bean salad 55
  Braised cabbage with bacon and nutmeg 100
  Braised radicchio and smoked mozzarella
    bruschetta 17
  Braised zucchini with olives 100
  Broiled asparagus 92
  Broiled eggplant with coriander and chili 51
  Carrots with cumin 96
  Deep-fried artichokes 95
  Eggplant with coriander and chili 51
  Eggplant with feta, sesame seeds and
    paprika, pan-fried 88
  Eggplant with sumac, roasted 99
  Fava beans with fresh cheese 80
  Frittata with bottarga and asparagus 83
  Green beans with tomatoes and basil 95
  Italian broccoli and broth soup 37
  Leeks with caper, parsley and anchovy
    sauce 55
  Lima beans with chorizo 30
  Marinated cauliflower and carrots with
    cumin and cardamom 59
  Pan-fried eggplant with feta, sesame
    seeds and paprika 88
  Patatas bravas 103
  Pumpkin with chili and nutmeg 96
  Roasted eggplant with sumac 99
  Saffron potatoes with red onions 103
  Spring vegetables with yogurt and mint 99
  Smoked eggplant purée 12
  Spinach and chickpea stew 69
  Vegetable platter 25
  Zucchini, pumpkin and red bell pepper
    al forno 92

Vegetable platter 25
vinegars 47

Wilted spinach with Serrano ham and eggs 84

yogurt 79

Zucchini, pumpkin and red bell
  pepper al forno 92
Zucchini salad with mint and chili, 55
Zucchini with olives, braised 100

STYLISH MEDITERRANEAN IN MINUTES